THE GUARDIANS

"Fast and furious . . . nonstop adventure!"
—Edward Bryant,
Mile High Futures

There is a plan for the day after.
It's called the blueprint.
And these are the men who will
make it happen . . .

Wilson—Expert pilot, sniper and mechanic. Flunked out of combat school for being too aggressive.

Sloan—Electronics and computer genius. Quick with gallows humor. Deadly with a grenade launcher.

Rogers—The group's medic and utility outfielder. He doesn't take prisoners.

McKay—The leader. His maximum experience in land warfare, urban combat and anti-terrorism made him a natural.

THE GUARDIANS
ARMAGEDDON RUN

RICHARD AUSTIN

A JOVE BOOK

THE GUARDIANS: ARMAGEDDON RUN

A Jove Book / published by arrangement with
the author

PRINTING HISTORY
Jove edition / April 1986

ISBN: 0-515-08598-7

Jove books are published by The Berkley Publishing Group,
200 Madison Avenue, New York, N.Y. 10016.
The words "A JOVE BOOK" and the "J" with sunburst
are trademarks belonging to Jove Publications, Inc.

PRINTED IN THE UNITED STATES OF AMERICA

THE GUARDIANS
ARMAGEDDON RUN

CHAPTER
ONE ————————————————

At their backs the sky burned red as hell.

"Everybody all right?" Billy McKay asked. The tiny microphone taped to his larynx picked up his words and conveyed them, via the personal communicator in the pocket of his silver-gray coveralls, to the little bone-conduction speakers taped behind the ears of his three teammates. The blacked-out deuce-and-a-half truck he was driving at reckless speed hit a bump in the red clay Iowa road. He grunted as his crew-cut head struck the metal roof of the cab.

"Couldn't be better, Billy," sang the boyish voice of Casey Wilson, who was steering the ten-metric-ton bulk of the Super Commando V-450 armored car they'd liberated across the darkened landscape with the fevered élan of an Indy driver.

"Roger that," echoed Tom Rogers. As punctuation he let off another shuddering burst from the car's formidable twin turret guns.

Driving the second deuce-and-a-half, Sam Sloan answered, "I'm fine, Billy. But Pirate"—a glance to the side—"he didn't make it."

"Shit." McKay glanced left into the wing mirror. Magenta and green tracers cut chords across the sky behind them.

1

Perhaps survivors of the Federated States of Europe forces—the FSE—were blazing away at the wild-eyed locals running through the woods around the flaming crater where the supersecret Heartland complex had been until a matter of minutes before. Or maybe they were shooting each other up; he didn't know. As long as nothing came *this* way. "All right. Form up on me, Sam. Case, you take the lead. Anybody chases us, you drop back and teach them better. But right now I want you up front."

"Where are we going?" Casey and Sergeant Marla Eklund asked simultaneously.

"Fucked if I know." A bullet struck the frame of the driver's side window, howling away like a scalded banshee. McKay grimaced. "Away from here. In a maximum hurry."

Sam Sloan was trying to look in all directions at once. The hero of Sidra Gulf had been trained for war in the steel confines of a warship like the *Winston-Salem*, the cruiser in which he'd won a Silver Star and brief notoriety several years before. This was definitely not his element. And the limp body of the biker and former Special Forces man known only as Pirate, which was slumped at his side, lurching into him with ghastly camaraderie at every bump, wasn't making him any happier. But Sloan didn't have the heart to reach over and open the passenger door and let the corpse go spilling out.

Ahead of him, first the armored car and then McKay's truck plunged into dark woods. Swallowing hard, Sloan followed. Into inky blackness. "Jesus, Casey," he yelled. *"Lights!"*

"No way, Sam. Somebody will see."

The skin was crawling on Sloan's neck and back as if it was trying to bunch up on top of his head, and his hands felt as if they were frozen to the steering wheel. Apparently that lunatic Casey was willing to go barreling through this cavernous blackness with no light at all. Sloan wasn't. He didn't have either Casey's eyesight or his leopard reflexes. Sam Sloan was a Guardian, but he wasn't a fool. He slowed, hoping he'd make it through these trees before the others pulled too far ahead.

"Sloan?" McKay's voice grunted in his ears. "You still got your IR goggles?"

He blinked. "Yes." The filtered spectacles he and the rest of the team had used to infiltrate the heavily guarded airshafts of the complex had been pushed up on top of his head, and in the excitement he totally forgot about them. He snapped them down as, at the head of the little convoy, Casey punched on the V-450's infrared headlights. Instantly the forest road became an otherworldly green tunnel, eerier by far than total blackness had been. And not a moment too soon. Almost at once the Super Commando was heeling over on its heavy-duty suspension as Casey cranked a hard right turn. Fishtailing, McKay followed, as did Sloan, spinning the wheel for all he was worth and thanking every god he'd ever heard of for the hazardous driving course he'd taken during Guardians training. As it was, his truck skidded fifteen meters broadside and came to a complete halt, leaning up against a low shoulder of slope spongy with fallen, rotting leaves.

With a sigh, the deuce-and-a-half settled back onto its springs. For a moment he sat there half-stunned, listening to little screaks and pings as the stressed metal of the truck frame sorted itself out again, the running grumble of the engine—with a distinctly asthmatic tone to it, now—and thumps and groans and muffled curses from the back as the dozen or so scientists and survivors of Marla Eklund's scratch platoon sorted *themselves* out. Sloan shook his head and got the truck moving again.

A thought struck him. "What about Callahan's people?" he asked. The biker band had parted company with them when the two trucks split up to pick up the survivors of India Three, promising to raise enough hell to keep any Effsees who still had the wits to muster off their butts.

"They'll find us or they won't," McKay growled. "Callahan's a big boy now."

Sloan grinned. The nose of his truck was a few meters behind McKay's tailgate. The ex-marine's vehicle was a rounded oblong blackness wallowing in the unearthly green tunnel. After the near-disaster at the curve, Casey was taking things at a more sedate pace—but one still manic enough to keep Sam Sloan's sweat and adrenaline flowing like the Arkansas River at flood.

"Just got a call from Dreadlock on the radio, Billy," Sloan

heard Casey say. "Said that he spotted us and is going to join us up." A moment later he saw a yellow-white light in his wing mirror, winking spasmodically like an eye with a tic, and then the roadway filled with lights as a dozen or more motorcycles crowded up behind.

He heard startled cries from the back of the truck. He stuck his head out the window and shouted, "Don't shoot! They're friends!" Then he ducked just in time to avoid being decapitated by a low-hanging branch. *Being a hero*, he reflected, *ain't all it's cracked up to be*.

"What do those bastards think this is," Billy McKay said, "spring break at Daytona Beach?" Even as he spoke a low-slung Harley chopper pulled up alongside the cab. The driver leaned over, way past the point of insane risk, to hammer three times on the door of the cab, then flashed a peace sign and a quick grin beneath a Fu Manchu mustache and World War I aviator's goggles. Sure enough, it was Dreadlock Callahan, his tangled mane flapping in the breeze.

McKay scowled at him, but the IR goggles hid the expression. "Anybody'd see those fucking lights for miles."

"Those boys don't have those cute little goggles like you-all," Eklund pointed out. "They've got to see where they're going. And with the trees this thick, nobody's going to see the lights very far—if anybody's even looking for us."

It would take an extraordinary hardness of core for any of the FSE bravos to be seriously hunting the team that had just blasted the vast Heartland Complex out of its artificial hill, McKay had to admit.

Casey was crowding it, hitting at least fifty klicks an hour—not very fast under most conditions, but on this backwoods track—ungraded for over a year—the wheel-ruts so deep that the differential of Sloan's truck kept thumping the hump in the middle of the road—it was pretty shaggy. These trees seemed to go on forever. Sloan was surprised; he didn't remember any huge stand of trees on the maps of the area he'd studied. Then again, he realized they hadn't been in the forest very long at all. Under pressure, time became difficult to measure. In a matter of seconds—that seemed like hours—they were out of the trees.

And running headlong into an FSE column.

Still rocking from side to side from the way Casey had throttled around the final dogleg, the V-450 rolled out into an open field and all but rammed a boxy M-113 armored personnel carrier head-on. Behind the track crept an ancient carryall and a pair of deuce-and-a-half army trucks with lights blacked out.

Casey jerked the wheel hard left with a yelp of surprise. There was a loud metallic bang as the snout of the APC clipped the car's right rear fender. Then the V-450 was turning along the side of the road, servos whining protest and burned hydraulic fluid stinking as Rogers fought to traverse the turret fast enough to bring the guns to bear.

Startled, the man in the M-113's cupola swung his .50-caliber around and triggered a burst. Green tracer streaks, like laser beams, cut just above the V-450's rear deck.

"Sam—break right!" McKay shouted, spinning his own wheel left to follow the armored car. Cat-quick, Marla Eklund poked her Close Assault Weapons System—usually known as CAWS—out the passenger window and began blasting full-auto at the fifty-gunner. The blast and tremendous yellow-white flashes of the souped-up twelve-gauge shotgun caught the man's attention. He started to swing his big machine gun to blast the truck to smithereens. A charge of Teflon-coated triple-aught buck caught him in the shoulder and neck and threw him back against the rim of the hatch. He slumped out of sight as the truck lurched past, swaying dangerously from side to side.

Even though she hadn't nearly exhausted the ten-round magazine by McKay's count, Eklund dropped it from its bay behind the single pistol grip and stuffed in a fresh clip from a pouch at her belt.

McKay's barked order to Sam Sloan was turning out not to have been such a hot idea. The former Navy commander had complied instantaneously, breaking to the other side of the caravan—just in time for the creaky International Harvester carryall, bolting away from the giant looming armored car, to ram it from the left front. Sloan heard a great grinding squeal, and his heart stopped as his truck heeled way, way over to the right at impact. Fortunately, the carryall was much the lighter vehicle, and not moving very fast. But Sloan heard screams from the rear of the truck, not all from fear alone.

Casey yelled at Tom Rogers to swing the turret left and then he gunned the big 450 for all she was worth. The ex-Green Beret had been busy traversing right, but without hesitation he instantly spun the turret counterclockwise. The Guardians were a team, and this was the way they worked: smoothly, effortlessly, unquestioningly. The armored car passed the last vehicle in line and then began plowing up the Iowa countryside in a tight circling turn to the left.

Sloan jacked into reverse and pumped the gas pedal of his truck, but the vehicle was stuck. The passenger door of the carryall had opened, and soldiers were beginning to spill out of the back; the occupants had begun to recover after being stunned. Sloan wrenched his own CAWS from under Pirate's lifeless body, poked it out the window, and let fly, blowing the windshield into the driver's face with his first shot.

Meanwhile, Marla Eklund was graphically demonstrating the rationale behind her flying magazine change. As McKay continued to churn overland toward the tail of the FSE convoy she aimed her CAWS at the rear gate of the M-113 just as it began to descend. Her first shot hit high and right with a bright hard flash like a miniature sun. It was a depleted-uranium round, the ultradense heavy-metal slug reacting with the aluminum armorplate of the APC in a violent chemical reaction that produced a burst of intense heat and light. She fired four more shots in rapid succession, putting three into the track's ramp, the slugs melting easily through the 13-millimeter armor to become blazing comets ricocheting violently around the track's insides. The APC slewed abruptly to its left, its treads tearing out great gouts of black earth and throwing them up in a bow wave like a destroyer at full speed ahead.

Halfway around Casey's circle, Rogers finally got the FSE convoy in the sights of his two turret guns. He held off on triggering the M-19 automatic grenade launcher, afraid that one of the white phosphorus rounds that alternated with High-Explosive Dual-Purpose rounds on the feed belt might splash Sam Sloan's stalled truck or the scientists and soldiers in the back of McKay's vehicle. On the other hand, there wasn't a thing in the world to prevent him raking the waddling M-113 with .50-caliber fire. The APC's armor was never designed to withstand that kind of punishment. Even over the rapidly developing firefight the people in the other two trucks could hear the sledgehammer banging of the massive slugs punching into the APC's hull.

The enemy track's top hatches popped and men began to tumble out. The tailgate finally dropped and a man stumbled out shrieking, wrapped in flames, flapping his arms like a maddened bird. He staggered several steps, illuminating the scene with a horrible light, and then the M-113 exploded.

Soldiers were spilling out of the two FSE trucks now, some of them to light out for the trees as fast as their legs could carry them, others to drop down by the roadside and open fire. They had a lot more targets than they could easily sort out. Dreadlock Callahan's people, who for all of their bravado hadn't hesitated to drop back behind the caravan to avoid being crushed by one of the half-blind giants lumbering through the woods, had now caught up and were streaming out to both sides of the stalled convoy. Afraid of hitting the bikers, Tom Rogers held his fire as Casey drove straight for the two stalled FSE trucks. Realizing the problem, Callahan scrambled his big chopper—unwieldy once off the pavement —across the field like a sheepdog, trying to herd his people out of the Guardians' field of fire.

Billy McKay heard an angry crackle from the rear of his truck as his passengers began to open up on the men bailing out into the road. This wasn't an ambush, this was a meeting engagement—one the Effsee bastards obviously weren't any more thrilled about than the Guardians. The obvious thing to do was just drive on. McKay was tempted to do just that, but as he cranked the big truck back onto the road behind the last FSE vehicle he finally had a chance to see the spot where Sam Sloan's truck lay locked in its unfortunate embrace with the Harvester carryall. "Sam!" he exclaimed. "Are you all right?"

"I'm fine, Billy." If it hadn't been for the bone-conduction speaker taped to the mastoid process behind his right ear, McKay would never have heard the soft Missouri twang above the noise of Eklund's CAWS as she blasted buckshot at the FSE troopies.

"Holy shit. Sam's stuck." Wrestling with the wheel, McKay faced a lightning decision. Getting as many of the rescued Blueprint personnel away clear was now top priority. But to just cruise on—with as yet no safe haven in mind—would leave Sam Sloan and the people he was carrying stuck in the middle of a developing firefight.

He made his choice. Finally back on the road, such as it was, McKay goosed the big truck toward an independent stand of trees alongside the road the FSE column had been following. He noticed that the thunder of Rogers's turret guns had stopped and knew at once why. In the fracas developing on the road, with Callahan's bikers milling around all over everywhere, Tom could no longer shoot without the almost certain risk of blowing away some of his own people.

"Casey, park that thing in some trees and let Tom cover what he can. Tom, keep an eye out to make sure no one else joins the party."

"Roger, Billy."

"I'm going to bail out and go help, Billy," Casey said.

McKay brought the truck to a grinding, shivering halt. *Why the fuck not?* Parking the armored car did make it a big fat juicy target, but they weren't talking an organized battle with serious possibilities of antitank fire here so much as a frantic, totally confused rumble.

"Roger that."

"McKay? MacGregor here. I've got a rifle; I'm coming too."

"Fuck a bunch of—I mean, negative, Mr. President." MacGregor's voice was warped way out of shape; he was obviously looking forward to getting some of his own back from the men who'd tortured him. *Got to think fast—if Jeff doesn't feel he's taking part, he's gonna come wading out into a bullet.* "You take the wheel. You can drive that beast, can't you?"

"I think so."

"Go for it. Please, sir." He turned to Eklund. "Let's go."

The sergeant jacked the last magazine into the CAWS's receiver and nodded at him. He had a quick flash of how beautiful she was with her close-cropped hair and big blue eyes, and a body that wouldn't stop even in her bulky fatigues, and how much he hated throwing her into the middle of this. But he didn't have a choice.

Besides, he had no way of making her stay behind, short of knocking her out and tying her up. And there just wasn't time for that.

CHAPTER
TWO ———————————————

Voices were calling from the canvas-covered rear of the truck, demanding to know why they were stopping. Down the road McKay saw the flash of a grenade near the wrecked vehicles. *Shit—Sam!* But he couldn't spare Sloan any worry.

Marla stuck her head in over the tailgate. "Young woman, what on earth is going on?" a man's voice inquired tremulously. "Why have we stopped?"

"Little matter of a firefight. Chi"—the name rhymed with *high*—"you get these folks out of this here truck and into the woods."

"Yes, Sergeant," the lanky Jimi Hendrix lookalike said from the darkness of the truck.

"But we've got guns!" said another male voice, considerably less timid if no steadier than the first. "Let us help!"

McKay winced. He had a vision of armed, vengeful amateurs running blindly into the middle of a point-blank battle—or simply spraying friend and foe alike with full-auto fire from up here in the trees. "No sir," Eklund said politely but breathlessly, "best way you can help us is to get out and keep your head down. Chi, make them *move*!"

McKay and Eklund ran off down the road. A clot of men

came running directly at them. They drove on, weapons ready. Ten meters on another grenade flash illuminated uniforms in a camo pattern neither recognized immediately—which made these enemies. A booming blast from Eklund's shotgun dropped one man kicking and writhing in the dirt. The others simply split to both sides and went streaming off into the fields like a herd of stampeding cattle.

"I'm sorry," Eklund said to the man she'd shot. They ran on.

In the cab of the wrecked truck, Sam Sloan was not having the time of his life. Behind him, James Tall Bear, the capable, taciturn Kiowa corporal who was Eklund's second in command, was trying to get the panicked scientists to safety while grenades popped all around them and bullets cracked past their ears. Whether they were unduly hard-core or just felt they were well and truly stuck in it, most of the Effsees riding the rammed carryall were hanging in to slug it out. That meant Sloan—crouched down behind the open door of the cab for what protection it offered—and the handful of India Three people in his truck were trading shots with the FSE expeditionary force troops at ranges down to less than ten meters.

Sam Sloan knew the range all too well. Seconds ago he'd seen a dazzling flash of muzzle blast so near he'd felt it, and both heard and felt a huge slamming impact that was a lot different from the pinpricks of 5.56 fire. Now he was living proof that the shot had been fired from less than ten meters—the arming range in flight of the 40-millimeter launched grenade that had dented his door. Sam had fired off the last five rounds in his magazine in a single automatic burst and the grenade launcher hadn't fired again. Of course, it might not have had time.

Miraculously, no one had actually thought to toss a grenade through the cracked front windshield. Yet.

"Sam? McKay. We're coming back to clean up on these bozos." In the hideous din Sloan could barely hear his leader. "Pull the hell out of here if you can so we know what we're shooting," McKay ordered.

"How's it going back there?" Sloan shouted over his shoulder.

"Got a lady scientist hung up on the tailgate, Commander," Tall Bear, always correct, shouted back. "We almost got her out."

"Hurry up. We have to pull back."

The problem with shouted communications was that it was a lot more easy for the enemy to overhear them. Or maybe the Effsees just decided to rush right about then. But even as Sloan was yelling to Tall Bear he saw figures come charging up toward the truck in the glare of the burning APC. Sloan fired a buckshot round through the window and realized to his chagrin that he had missed. The second trigger pull brought no response at all; he'd just fired the last round of his last magazine. His little jaunt inside Heartland hadn't left him much of an ammunition load for a full-dress firefight.

He dropped the useless CAWS and ripped his big shiny Python .357 Magnum from his shoulder holster. A shadowy figure suddenly lunged around the open door. Sloan shot the man in the chest at such close range it set the front of his camouflage blouse ablaze, then turned and sprinted for the rear of the vehicle. He heard the ugly little cracking, ripping sounds of supersonic bullets passing him, and then the thump and crash of broken glass he'd been dreading for the last endless minute. He threw himself on the ground as the cab of the truck exploded. He pulled himself up and dashed forward—straight into a withering blast of gunfire.

Twisting, he fell back to the ground. Tall Bear was roaring for his men to hold their fire. India Three, hardened by a year's survival in after-the-Holocaust land, instantly stopped shooting. But one of the scientists froze on the trigger of an M-16, raking the grass around Sloan's prostrate form. Tall Bear ran to him and kicked the long black rifle spinning from his hands, then grunted and fell heavily as an FSE bullet found him.

Sloan twisted around. The fusillade mistakenly directed at him had halted his pursuers by the burning cab. The scientists and the remnants of India Three were belly down in the grass ten or twenty meters behind the truck. Sloan rolled over behind a rear tire, hoping the gas tank wouldn't blow anytime soon, and opened fire with his .357 Magnum. Its thundering noise and kicking recoil somehow didn't seem really significant against the general din of battle.

He was vaguely aware of Callahan's bikers buzzing around in the background, taking occasional potshots, and had a fleeting impression of a number of the bikers simply peeling away and fleeing into the darkness. They'd done well keeping the attention of Heartland's security forces directed outward, and he'd been impressed with the way they hung together during the withdrawal from the smoking ruin of Heartland itself. Now the shock of having run smack into the enemy after believing themselves safely away was just too much for a number of them. But not all—including, he guessed, the irrepressible Dreadlock Callahan.

A lone bike came weaving past the burning M-113 in among the stalled vehicles, its skinny, bare-chested rider blazing away to both sides with a chopped-down autoloading shotgun. He almost made the rear of the wrecked carryall before a volley of shots knocked him down. Not all the bikers were running, no.

"Sam?" Casey asked. "Are you away from the truck?"

Sloan wasn't, really, but he knew what Casey meant and this was no time to quibble. "Yes," he said. As he spoke, he felt something small but heavy hit the ground not far from his head and bounce twice. He stuck his head behind the tire, pressed his face to earth, and prayed.

Light and sound enveloped him. For a moment he lay there stunned, aware of no sensation at all. Then he made himself roll to his right, bringing up the Python before him in both hands. There were men rushing him in the eerie silence, flame and starlight glinting off the Buck Rogers shapes of little Austrian Steyr AUG assault rifles. He shot one. He felt the recoil, but heard no sound of a shot. *My eardrums are gone*, he thought, as the man went over backward onto the earth, throwing his rifle into the air. A second man stopped and aimed his rifle right smack at the center of Sam's forehead. Frantically, Sam tried to switch targets.

Then his assailant dropped to his knees and pitched forward onto his face. Without pausing to wonder about his miraculous deliverance, Sam swung the vented barrel of the Python to shoot the next man in the gut. The fourth man, hanging to the rear, turned and darted back the way he'd come. He made it three steps and collapsed like a marionette with the strings snipped.

A miracle named Casey Wilson had saved Sam Sloan. Somewhere in the grass on the other side of the stalled convoy Casey lay on his belly, sniping with single shots of his silenced MP-5. It wasn't that the former fighter jock was afraid to mix in a face-to-face brawl—the only reason Casey knew the meaning of the word *fear* was because he'd picked up a good vocabulary at school—but he knew he was far more effective in this role.

Shadow movement to his right caught Sloan's peripheral vision. He snapped the big chrome-plated Python around, pulled the trigger. Even without the use of his ears it was painfully apparent that a lot of nothing happened. Sam Sloan's last thought was that McKay had been right about him all along, and that just like a greenhorn he'd gotten caught up in firefight fever and forgotten to count his rounds.

Then Marla Eklund was crouching down beside him, shaking his shoulder, her mouth working as she tried to speak to him. Grinning sheepishly, thinking about how bad he'd feel if he'd shot Sergeant Eklund by accident—*especially* after Billy McKay caught him—he pointed to his ear with his left hand. Holding her big CAWS in her right hand, Eklund nodded, pointing back toward where her men and the scientists were lying in the grass. It seemed to Sloan that she was suppressing a smile. He attributed it to shell shock.

Billy McKay had gotten in among the stalled vehicles of the convoy like a wolf in the fold. He'd fired his MP dry; even though the six-foot-three, two-hundred-forty-pound marine could haul a weapons load that would founder a mule, and even though he'd mostly fired his little Heckler and Koch machine pistol on single shot in the fortress, those things got awfully thirsty when the hammer came down for true. He fired his last round into the belly of an officer type who popped up from the ditch beside the last truck in line and appropriated the man's Uzi submachine gun. Then he just moved forward, hunkering low, shooting everything that moved while hoping none of his friends lurking out in the darkness would shoot *him*.

It was the kind of fight every smart soldier hated in his bones, no matter how battle-hardened or special warfare-trained: a fight where good guys and bad were mixed together like M&M's in a bag. Usually in such circumstances you shot at anything that moved and hoped for the best, but Billy McKay was relying on senses, reflexes, and instincts honed way past razor sharpness by a thousand firefights to keep all the good guys—himself included—in one piece. This was Billy McKay's element, had been since the days he was a street-fighting kid in Pittsburgh.

He moved forward by short rushes, pausing at the tailgate of the stalled rear truck to spray the inside with a quick burst. No response; he snapped around the end and caught a bare-headed trooper creeping up at him along the truck silhouetted in the glare from the burning track. He dropped the man and moved forward. A little ways beyond he saw men clustered at the back of the stalled carryall and sprayed them with fire. Three went down, and then a Honda scrambler bike streaked behind them, rider leaning over to split one's skull with a tomahawk in passing. The others ran away.

The biker spun his Honda in a shower of dirt, looked at McKay with weird blazing eyes from under the filthy rag knotted around his head. His face and naked upper torso were blackened with soot, streaked with sweat. He glared a moment, then jumped the bike forward. *Oh God, I'm going to have to shoot the puke,* McKay thought in disgust. *He don't recognize me.*

He was fifteen meters from McKay and the hatchet was just coming up when a red flower blossomed right in the center of the black-smeared chest. The biker tumbled off over the rear wheel. McKay took a long step away from the shelter of the truck, pivoted, brought the Uzi up, and fired a three-round burst from the hip. The FSE soldier standing on top of the truck screamed, dropped his AUG, and fell bent over to the dirt at McKay's side.

McKay moved forward to where the nose of the second truck had rammed up against the tailgate of the other. If there was anyone left in this truck, they weren't showing themselves either. He started to slip cautiously toward the gap where the carryall had swung out of line from behind the stricken M-113. Then something, some vagrant hint of danger, tickled his senses. He spun, Uzi at the ready.

Dreadlock Callahan stood there, poised on the locked

bumpers of the trucks. In his hands he held a Smith and Wesson 3000 pump shotgun, which he usually carried in a scabbard on his bike for occasions when he thought something more authoritative than his Ruger Redhawk .44 was called for. Like this one. The lanky, light-skinned black took his eternal brown cigarillo from his mouth. "It's a good thing," he remarked, "that you've got reflexes as good as mine."

It was all over, as the saying goes, but the shouting. Whatever the FSE column had been up to, it was painfully apparent that they hadn't been expecting a fight, and had wanted one even less. The tenacity of the soldiers in the wrecked carryall had probably been no more than a cornered-rat response.

As soon as the firing died down, Casey slipped back to relieve Tom in the turret of the V-450 while Rogers moved to the road to help some of the more medically inclined Blueprint personnel tend the wounded.

Only one of the Blueprint people had been killed—oddly enough a passenger in McKay's truck rather than Sloan's—but three were wounded in Sam's. Additionally, the quiet young woman called Gillet had been shot up in the fight at the carryall, as well as Tall Bear.

Having ordered Sloan and the rest of India Three to secure the area, Billy McKay was standing around wishing ferociously for a cigar when he was suddenly hit from two directions. From his right came a bruised, weeping blond teenaged girl dressed only in a white-and-red football jersey who wrapped herself around his neck like a bolo and clung. From the other direction clumped Marguerite Connoly, Ph.D., looking grim in stained Pendleton shirt and hiking boots.

The blonde wailed in McKay's ears like a stuck air horn. He nodded over her death grip at the economist. "Doctor," he choked.

Connoly stared at the girl's bare white rump, exposed where her jersey rode up in back. The economist's eyebrows crawled up into view from behind thick round spectacles. "Lieutenant McKay, if you can spare some attention from this . . . un-fortunate . . . young woman for a moment—"

"Fire away, Doc." McKay knew the girl had been through a terrible ordeal as sex slave to the mad Trajan—the Guardians' old nemesis, head of the postwar Central Intelligence Agency and Yevgeny Maximov's viceroy for the United States of America—in Heartland. But he was still just about ready to coldcock her. This was getting embarrassing. Nothing like this ever happened to Sergeant Rock. Not even to Clint Eastwood.

Using all his massive strength he managed to loosen her arms enough to allow him to breathe and get the bare soles of her feet back on the ground. Connoly, damn her, was looking at him as if *he'd* been the one to have her chained to his bedroom wall in Heartland. "Lieutenant McKay, are you aware that that—that motorcycle gang is murdering the prisoners?" she asked.

Almost invisible in the firelight, McKay's brows rose. "Prisoners? We didn't take no prisoners."

"I see. Then they're simply murdering the wounded, is that it?" The irony was thick enough McKay could have cut it with his Ka-bar.

"What do you expect, lady?" he rasped. "They're motorcycle outlaws, not the Sisters of Mercy."

"I simply can't understand how you can permit such things to happen under your command—"

"They're *not* under my command. They're just giving us a hand." Actually, Dreadlock's Desperadoes were mercenaries, and their fees for taking part in this action were being picked up by some of the Freeholders back in Colorado as their contribution toward fighting the FSE expeditionary force.

"How do you feel you can possibly rebuild America using such criminal elements—"

"Now, just what in the heck is going on here?" McKay's heart sank lower. Standing in front of him like a shabby avenging angel, her uniform scorched and tattered, her face smeared with remnants of blackout, her plush-cut hair standing out in spiky little tufts from sweat and greasepaint, Marla Eklund was staring hard at the half-naked teenager fixed to Billy McKay's bull neck. *Great,* he thought, *just great. Five minutes ago I'm a hero, and now some economist thinks I'm a child molester and this damned Texan lady sergeant is going to shove her CAWS up my butt.*

But Eklund's furious face was softening. "Why, the poor child. She's *terrified.*"

"That's what I been trying to tell you."

"You poor thing. Come on, honey, let's get you back in the truck." Mother-gentle, Eklund disentangled the girl and led her away. The blonde kid—whose name was Sally—was maybe not as helpless as the sergeant thought, McKay knew. During the attack on Heartland she had become so hysterical at the prospect of Trajan's abusing her more that she'd picked up a chair and beaten his head to jelly with it. But this wasn't the time to point that out.

Connoly was still bitching at him, but he tuned her out. "Tom."

"Yo, Billy."

"How are you coming with those wounded?"

"Done pretty much what we can. Tall Bear's walking. Gillet needs more attention than we can give her here, and so do a couple of the folks you rescued."

"Roger. Je—Mr. President, will you please drive the car down to the road? You can use the headlights. Anybody's looking for us, they're going to know how to find us by now. Casey, you stay up in the turret and keep an eye on things." He looked around and saw the aftermath of yet another battle. "Listen up, everybody. It's time for us to saddle up and go."

"Yo, McKay," called Rosie, one of Eklund's people. The stocky black had had his forearm laid open by a bullet but wasn't paying it any mind. "But where're we gonna go?"

McKay grinned. There was really just one answer, but it had taken him a little while to think of it. "Rosie, my man, you're about to make the acquaintance of the fleshpots of scenic Luxor, Iowa."

They made the trip without incident. Probably no one was looking for them. The FSE expeditionary force troops who'd been stationed in and around Heartland had seen their high command and most of their buddies blown skyward in a huge orange fireball. They had enough on their plates without worrying about a bunch of raggedy-ass refugees.

The Guardians and Jeff MacGregor knew the road to Luxor quite well, only from the other direction. In the blazing days after the One-Day War the small farming community had been their last stop on their run to Heartland from a shattered Washington, D.C. A breakdown of Mobile One, their original V-450, had required McKay and Sloan to hike overland to a cache—laid down before the War as part of preparations for putting Project Blueprint into effect—for spare parts.

But the cache had been discovered and blown open by National Guardsmen commanded by Major General Rodey Westerfield. Westerfield and his men, along with certain elements of the Iowa State Patrol, had taken over the town in the hours following the thermonuclear exchange. They had clamped a reign of terror on the town, ruling by iron fist, taking what they wanted and killing everyone who stood in their way. In order to repair Mobile One and get President Jeff MacGregor to the safety of Heartland, the Guardians had been compelled to make common cause with the townsfolk—in the face of strict prohibition by Major Crenna against getting involved in local affairs—to overthrow the renegade general.

Casey led off now in the liberated V-450, McKay behind him, and then the people from Sam Sloan's truck loaded in the two abandoned FSE deuce-and-a-halfs, which they'd stuffed with all the weapons, ammo, and gear they could scarf or scavenge. It was less than an hour to Luxor even over the weathered, unmaintained back-country roads they had to take to avoid major arteries clotted with rusting auto hulks. Toward Luxor, the flat Iowa farmland began to take on a slight variation, like a slow ocean swell. "Just another klick or so, Billy," Casey said over their commlink. "Don't see any lights from town, yet."

"At least," Sam Sloan said as they crested a rise, "we're assured of a friendly reception this time."

As if on cue, the road to either side of the Super Commando exploded with magenta fire, bathing the convoy in light and illuminating a truck blocking the road not thirty meters ahead.

CHAPTER
THREE ────────────────

"What the fuck?"

"Ambush, Billy. I think I can bust it," Casey said. He rammed the accelerator to the deck.

"No!" Billy McKay bellowed, loud enough to make Marla Eklund wince as she pointed her scrounged Steyr suspiciously at the barricade. He could hear the roar of the Desperadoes' cycle engines as they scrambled off the road into the comforting blackness. Behind him, he heard excited voices, the rattle of rifle bolts being cocked. "Just hold on, Case, Tom. Let's see what's going down here."

The other Guardians acknowledged. The truck rocked slightly on its suspension. "My people are bailing out the back," Marla Eklund said. McKay stuck his head out the open window and looked back. She was right. India Three's troopies were not about to be jacklighted in the middle of a road on top of half-full gas tanks.

"Hold it right there!" a young voice, amplified by a bullhorn, bellowed out from the barricade. "Everybody stay where they are or we'll open fire."

Someone here was being awfully ballsy. Something in that voice, young as it was, told McKay its owner could back up

20

those words—and meant to. But it still took an awful lot of guts to talk back to the awesome muzzles of a .50-caliber machine gun and a 40-millimeter automatic grenade launcher.

McKay opened his door and stepped out into the road. "Awright, everybody just *hold on!* India Three, at ease." He felt naked standing out there in the middle of that weird rosy glow. "You up there. We're bound for Luxor. We don't mean any trouble."

He heard scattered sounds of what he took to be dissension and skepticism from up behind the parked truck, which was an old rump-sprung Chevy with a wooden flatbed. Big chunks of broken cement had been piled on the bed to weigh it down and make it hard to bulldoze out of the way. It was a trick he'd encountered many times before in postwar America. If you've got something good, go with it.

"Who the hell you trying to fool? If you're so friendly, why do you got that damn armored car?"

"They got FSE markings on them trucks, Carl," somebody else called out, unamplified.

"We've dealt with your kind before. We ain't afraid of you, or your armored car either."

McKay's bellow had frozen soldiers and scientists in the act of leaping out of the three trucks. A couple had gone ahead and dived into the ditch. Others stood peering somewhat wild-eyed from the tailgates. "Listen," he said, starting to get hot under the collar, "we're *friends.* We been to this burg before, and the last time we helped haul your asses out of a pretty heavy-duty jam."

"Yeah, Carl," another young voice said. "We seen a car like that before—"

"Shut up, Randy. Just who the hell are you, mister?"

That voice was beginning to sound very familiar to Billy McKay. "I'm Lieutenant William McKay," he shouted back, "and we're the Guardians."

A pause hung, as heavy as the hot, humid night air. Then a young man stepped around the corner of the parked truck into the fading light from the flares tied to stakes on either side of the road. McKay had first seen his face above the vented barrel of a shotgun. "Well why didn't you say so earlier?" he said. He had an ancient U.S. Army M3-A1 grease gun hung around his neck by an Israeli-style sling improvised from army-surplus webbing—in apparent imitation of the Guardians' weapon slings. "I'm Carl Ledoux, Jr." He stepped forward, hesitated a moment, then stuck out his hand. McKay shook it, and suddenly he grinned.

From suspicion, the Luxorians' attitude snapped to uproarious welcome. A round-cheeked man with a white-blond mustache and a CAT hat fired up the Chevy's engine and moved the giant truck creaking off the road as the rest of the roadblock team swarmed forward to greet the newcomers.

Luxor remembered the Guardians, all right.

The Blueprint people and Eklund's troopers looked stunned as the half dozen townsfolk—four men and two women—surrounded them, hugging them and slapping backs. Tom and Casey were cajoled out of the V-450 briefly, and then the locals were startled when the President of the United States himself stepped out to shake their hand with a smile and cheery nod. That last wasn't good security, but if any FSE people were even *thinking* about them, they'd already have a pretty good idea that MacGregor—if he wasn't dead in Heartland—would be with the Guardians.

Besides, the plan was most definitely not to keep MacGregor under wraps. In these troubled times, America needed visible evidence of leadership. The priority was to get MacGregor someplace he could safely be seen by Americans.

Shaking young Carl Ledoux's hand across his grease gun, McKay noted the change that had come over the youth in the last year—though it had probably been accomplished even before the Guardians departed from their first visit, when the boy was wounded in his own living room fighting to defend his household and the new President of the United States from Westerfield's men. He had the look of weary self-confidence that comes from having been taken under fire and stood up, and survived.

McKay also noticed a blocky redheaded girl, who couldn't have been out of her teens, standing off to one side. She was hanging negligently on to the pistol grip of an RPG-7v antitank rocket launcher. It was a Soviet-bloc jobbie, and God only knew where they had gotten it, but it would've been more than sufficient to peel open the armor of a Super Commando.

No wonder Carl Junior had felt confident of his ability to deal with the armored car.

Conspicuously excluded from the welcome were Callahan's hardcases. The people of Luxor were straight, solid country folk, not the type who ever would've cottoned to bikers. And unless they were a lot luckier than anyone else who lived near a paved strip of road, they'd had at least one or two occasions since the War to revise their opinions downward. Callahan himself had been an up-front outlaw at one time, until he and his people got dragooned into the Crusade for the New Dispensation by Trajan's bone-breaking Brothers of Mercy. His reformation, however far it extended, wasn't exactly apparent on the surface of him. The bikers hung back, idling their engines and making comments. They kept them low, however.

The introductions over, everybody piled back into trucks. One of the sentries had already radioed news of the Guardians' return to town. Carl and the redhead, who'd exchanged her launcher for a basic lever-action Winchester, would ride in with them on horseback.

"Randy," Carl Junior called sharply. His shorter, stockier brother looked around with guilt on his young face. He'd wandered back to get a look at these funny two-wheeled critters in exotic drag, and had gotten very wrapped up in a conversation with a platinum-blond girl biker who couldn't have been that much older than he was. Randy bit his lip and trotted back. Shaking his head, Carl swung up onto his sorrel and led off.

They drove through deserted, darkened streets. Remembering the last time they'd been down these tidy avenues of well-kept whitewashed houses, each Guardian felt a prickle of the hairs on the back of his neck. They had played a deadly game with the town's occupiers, a game that culminated in a blazing firefight at the elementary school that Westerfield had appropriated as headquarters. But tonight felt different. Then the air had been charged with tension like heat lightning. Now, after all that the Guardians and those they'd rescued had been through, the darkened town felt like an oasis of serenity and calm.

In the center of town a lot of sleepy-looking citizens greeted them by the light of kerosene lanterns. Included in the reception committee were a stocky man with white sideburns introduced as Chief Sinclair and a tall, youthful-looking man introduced as the new mayor, Byron Jones. Also on hand were Carl and Randy's parents, Carl Senior and Sally. Theirs was the first house the Guardians had arrived at when they came to Luxor, and it had served as their base of operations throughout the brief struggle against the encroaching National Guard.

By this time McKay and company were staggering as reaction and exhaustion set in with a vengeance. Several volunteers, including the town nurse, began to settle the Blueprint scientists and India Three in the same school that, ironically, had been Westerfield's headquarters. McKay himself was so completely ragged out he could barely stand up; none of the introductions made much impression on him. He and Marla Eklund waved bleary good-byes at one another, and then the Guardians and President MacGregor followed the Ledoux's battered white Ford station wagon to their farm on the southeastern outskirts of the town.

Jeff MacGregor got the guest bedroom, and even though Sally tried to insist on driving her brood into their bedrolls, the four Guardians declined and unrolled their own sleeping bags out in the yard next to the cooling bulk of the V-450. Never particularly picky about where he slept, Billy McKay at the moment felt as if he could rack out on the bleachers in the middle of Super Bowl. He was asleep almost as soon as he stretched out.

Preparations were laid for a real old-fashioned winging the next night to celebrate the Guardians' triumphant return. Triumphant, because they had dealt the occupying forces of the FSE—who had made themselves massively unpopular in the months since their arrival—a telling blow. They had successfully infiltrated the most impregnable fortress in the North American continent. And they had rescued the President of the United States.

There was something about the admiration they won for that last feat that struck McKay as funny, once he and the others pried themselves out of the sack in the late morning and sat down to a massive country-style breakfast. In the months between the One-Day War and the FSE takeover, Jeff Mac-Gregor had had a major problem trying to get anybody to take him seriously. Local authorities all too frequently resisted the notion of a higher authority; they liked being on the tops of their little heaps. A lot of people still felt "Wild Bill" Lowell was the true and rightful President. For the most part the military—which had loved Lowell as its own—adopted a wait-and-see attitude toward the man who was by law their Commander in Chief. And most people the Guardians encountered in their travels across America frankly didn't seem to give a damn.

Occupation changed all that. In his first days back in office, Bill Lowell had elicited a public response greater than anything his onetime vice president had approached. The military in its isolated bases and holdouts was solidly behind him. Local leaders—like Kansas City's Dexter White—had rushed to acknowledge him. Even a number of small-time authority figures who'd set themselves up as satraps of their domains suddenly woke up and acknowledged him. Either they felt he had a better claim to legitimacy than MacGregor, or they feared he was one hell of a lot more likely to come down on them hard if they didn't toe the line. What had hurt Jeff MacGregor most was that the American people—the real folk, not the movers and the shakers but the masses—*they* were behind Bill Lowell.

At first.

Then the FSE gloves began to come off. The man behind the entire plan—the man who worked Bill Lowell's strings—Yevgeny Maximov, had no enormous expectation of actually seizing and holding the North American continent with his ten-thousand-man expeditionary force. Not even with that tremendous figurehead, the old bull Lowell himself. Maximov's goal was to strip America of what resources his men could plunder, grab, or pry up—and the most significant of all was the Blueprint for Renewal.

The Federated States of Europe—as Maximov's empire was known—were beginning to unravel. They needed American loot to pull through, and most of all they needed the Blueprint. Maximov was a man who loved power. But he was no fool. He wanted the United States if he could get it, that went without saying. But he knew all too well that he had first to secure his hold on Europe. The key to that was the Blueprint.

So the expeditionary force descended on the survivors of America like a horde of locusts. And Americans began to discover that playing cowboys and Indians isn't so much fun when you're the Indian.

None of this had done Wild Bill Lowell's public image a whole lot of good. And Jeff MacGregor, to judge by the response of the people of Luxor to his presence in their midst, was reaping the benefits of his late predecessor's massive popularity slip.

Early afternoon found the Guardians with the distinctly unglamorous task of routine maintenance. Tom Rogers—medium height, brown hair, built like a cinderblock and about as talkative—was stripping down the two big guns in the Super Commando's turret and cleaning them with the meticulous care of an operating room nurse handling the tools of a famous neurosurgeon. Casey Wilson—highest-scoring American fighter ace since the Korean War, a tall, lanky kid with a surfer's tan and sunbleached yellow hair—was in back of the V-450's passenger compartment with the access plate off, making sure the Heartland techs who had prepped this vehicle for whatever purpose had done the job right. Up front in the Electronic Systems Operator's seat, Sam Sloan was checking out the vehicle's communications, sensory, and computer gear. He was a long spare specimen with a shock of brown hair and a ready James Garner grin. A real down-home Missouri country boy who could kick shit with the best of them—and an honors graduate of the Annapolis Naval Academy who could ice over a duchess with sheer imperiousness if he had to. Billy McKay was rummaging through the vehicle's stores to see just what they'd gotten away with.

Jeff MacGregor was off hobnobbing with Mayor Jones and some of the other local politicos. The Blueprint people were all out at the school conferring with the townsfolk. It had been decided that they would remain here while the Guardians and MacGregor pushed on. The surplus weapons, ammo, and medical and communications supplies looted from the FSE convoy had gone a long way toward ensuring their acceptance by people whose natural country hospitality was still a little off from having been badly abused by Westerfield and company. Not that it would take that much to make the people of Luxor accept the Blueprint folk. A group of the top experts in their respective fields, assembled for the express purpose of masterminding the rebuilding of war-ravaged America, did not exactly make a shabby addition to any community.

Eklund and her people were busy elsewhere too, probably with the same soldier's chore as the Guardians. Marla had gently but firmly insisted that Sally—Sally from Heartland, that is—stay close to her. Left to her own devices, the girl tended to stick to Billy McKay as if she were grafted to his hip. The girl made sullen protest, which Eklund put a stop to with her best drill-sergeant manner (even a highly critical McKay had to admit it was pretty damn good). The stare she gave McKay as she went off with giant Jamake and several of her other people, and blond Sally casting longing glances back over her skinny shoulder, said that she didn't for one second blame this poor child for acting the way she was, but she wouldn't be one darn bit surprised if Billy McKay ravished the girl the first chance he got.

McKay and Eklund were having one of those strange, mostly silent periods again. Since any other kind of relationship between the two of them was a relatively new development, McKay wondered why it got to him so much. But it did.

"What I don't understand," Sam Sloan said, keying the initiating sequence for a computerized check of the radar systems into his console, "is how the folks hereabouts act as if the War had never happened. Oh, I can see differences, plenty of them. People walk and ride horses a lot more than they used to. Don't use electricity unless they have to. There's a whole lot more improvisation going on. But it's the way people *act*. It all seems too—too normal, somehow."

Tom Rogers climbed down from the turret to spread the M-2 machine gun's bolt/firing pin assembly on a square of oilcloth and go to work on it with Break-free. "Life goes on, Sam," he said.

Sloan turned around, mouth opened to zap Rogers for the

banality of the remark. He bit it off short. Tom Rogers didn't exactly fill Sam Sloan's bill as an intellectual, but Sloan knew his teammate to be a long way from stupid. And as soon as he dispensed with the reflexive flip remark, his forehead began to crease thoughtfully.

"What your problem is, Sam," McKay said, opening a locker filled with freeze-dried rations, "is that you watch too many of them damned nuclear-scare flicks from the eighties. The kind where, once the bomb's dropped, all the survivors get too depressed to get out of goddamned bed in the morning."

"Yeah, man," Casey Wilson offered. "And they all forget about things like engineering and medicine and modern agricultural techniques, and start, like, wearing furs and shooting each other with bows and arrows."

Sloan managed a sore laugh. "I don't know as I'm quite as impressionable as that. But you've probably got a point."

"Now, here's something interesting."

"What's that, McKay?" Sloan asked.

"The meals in this locker here. Others got, you know, just regular food. This one there's all this organic shit. Sprouts and tofu and like that. Ain't a gram of good red meat in here."

"So the car wasn't waiting for *us*," Sloan said sardonically. "But we sort of knew that already." None of the Guardians was a vegetarian.

"This thing is, like, right off the showroom floor, Billy," Casey said. "Parts are only worn enough to show they've been given a thorough checkout. What was it doing down in the main garage, anyway?"

"Probably intended to send out a team of their own," Tom Rogers said.

"One with a damned vegetarian on it," McKay said.

"You know, Billy," Casey Wilson said, his head buried once again inside the engine compartment, "what are we going to call this thing anyway?"

"I'll be happy enough to call it home, myself," Sloan remarked, keeping an eye on amber figures flashing up on the computer screen. "After all those months scraping by as best we could. Reliable transportation, firepower, hot meals, air conditioning—"

"Armor plate," McKay remarked. Sloan grinned; he was a Navy line officer by training, a cruiser man by experience.

"I feel just buck naked any other way," he admitted.

"So what are we going to call it?" Casey persisted.

"Can't call it Mobile Two," McKay said. "We had a Mobile Two. Never made it past Indiana." McKay wasn't a particularly superstitious man, but he never believed in tempting fate.

Casey scratched the hair at the back of his neck. For detailed work inside he was making the concession of not wearing his otherwise inevitable yellow Zeiss shooting glasses. "We could, like, do what the military does. Give it a variant number."

"Mobile One A-1," said Rogers, and, "Mobile One E-1," Billy McKay said, simultaneously.

"I was thinking more on the lines of Mobile One-B," Casey said, following Air Force naming procedure as the others were doing for Army and Marine Corps. "Maybe we should just go ahead and call it Mobile One. That's simplest."

McKay and Rogers looked at each other. "What the fuck?" McKay said. "You got a deal." Rogers nodded.

"That's not exactly what I'd call an imaginative name," Sloan said grumpily.

McKay flipped the food locker shut. "Yeah, if you think about it, Mobile One has a real ring to it, you know?"

"No."

McKay glowered. "Then how about I'm the commander of this sorry outfit, and also I'm a shitload bigger than you, and *I* like the name Mobile goddamn One!"

For a moment they glared at each other like strange dogs meeting on the street. Then Sloan laughed. "Hearts and minds, McKay. Hearts and minds."

"Grab 'em by the balls and their hearts and minds'll follow," McKay growled, voicing the credo that had made him the despair of every Special Forces trooper he'd ever worked with. "Mobile One it is."

Sloan sighed and turned back to the screen. The self-test had terminated; all systems were go. He started poking at the keys, half at random, still steamed at McKay's high-handed behavior.

He froze. "Billy, Case, take a look at this."

McKay squinted at the screen. Computers had been part of Guardians training, but they were never going to be his strong suit. It made no sense to him.

Casey though, wiping his hands on a flannel rag, started nodding and humming down in the back of his throat. "This what I think it is, Sam?"

If Casey's mellow surface had begun to ripple with excitement, Sloan was practically vibrating. "Hell yes. This damned car's got the code keys and recognition signals for the whole damned Federated States of Europe expeditionary force in its database!"

CHAPTER
FOUR ————————————————

"The way I see it, Mr. President," Billy McKay said, "is like this. We've got to get you somewhere safe, first off."

Sloan settled himself back on the threadbare sofa in the Ledoux's living room and took another sip of the sun tea Sally Ledoux had brought in on the yellow plastic tray. "You should also go somewhere with reasonable access to supplies—food and water, especially. And transportation. If you can, you should find someplace with a reasonably central location."

It was later in the afternoon. Some clouds had come up, but Carl Ledoux said that he didn't reckon it'd rain, or at least not enough to spoil the party set for that evening. The Guardians and President MacGregor were sitting around their hosts' living room. The Ledoux kids had all been sent off elsewhere; Carl Senior was working in the fields. Sally herself was out in the kitchen busying herself with chores. She assured them she wouldn't listen to a word they said, and even as paranoid as they had gotten about security, they believed her. And this was definitely for their ears only; even allies like Eklund, Dreadlock Callahan, and the Blueprint scientists had been excluded from this conference.

Sitting in an easy chair, MacGregor nodded slowly. "And I assume you gentlemen had suggestions in mind?" He didn't look like someone who'd been held prisoner for five months, often under conditions reminiscent of the Hanoi Hilton. Or like a man rescued literally within days of his own execution. The people in town had fixed him up with an honest-to-God suit, two-piece in blue, with black tie and black shoes and a shirt you could use to advertise Cheer. Jeans, hiking boots, and work shirt were more MacGregor's style, but he had accepted the offering and worn it with gratitude and pleasure. He was a politician born and bred, after all. Also, he was a hell of a nice guy. MacGregor looked very pulled together, laid-back without seeming drifty or sloppy. He looked for the most part as he always had, but somehow not even Billy McKay could any longer think of him as *just* a pretty-boy politician. Those months of captivity, of living without hope, had done something to him. Like burning fat off his spirit, McKay thought. Jeff MacGregor had emerged from his experience changed, something different. A leader, maybe.

McKay sure hoped so.

Sloan nodded. "We can write off Chicago. It got hit pretty hard during the War, and what's left is being fought over by FSE troops and home-grown rebels. And we're not too happy about any place on the East Coast; the whole seaboard got pretty well plastered. The South isn't central and we'd have a hard time finding surviving facilities that would be sufficient."

A wry grin quirked the corner of MacGregor's mouth. "I don't exactly want to be seen as a successor to Jeff Davis, even if he is something of a namesake."

"Be careful what you say, suh," Sam Sloan said in an exaggerated drawl. "Ah happen to be a Southern gentleman myself."

He took another sip of tea. "Actually, gentlemen," Jeff MacGregor said, "I think our choice is obvious."

Sloan's eyebrows rose. "What's that, sir?" McKay asked.

"Kansas City."

The Guardians looked at each other. McKay slowly crossed his arms across his chest. The sleeves of his silver-gray fatigue jumpsuit were rolled up, and his forearms looked gnarled as tree trunks. "Well, Mr. President," Sam Sloan said, worrying his underlip briefly with his upper teeth, "we've discussed that option in some depth among ourselves. And I have to admit KC has a lot to recommend it."

MacGregor nodded vigorously. "It's got everything we could ask for. It's in as central a location as is possible to have. It has transportation and water, and the farms around provided food. Best of all, there is a well-established, smoothly functioning civil authority." He waved a hand in the air. "It's ideal."

"Except for just one little thing, Mr. President," McKay said. MacGregor cocked an eyebrow at him. "The place is crawling with Effsees. And Dex White is in their back pocket."

MacGregor's eyebrows and mouth tensed slightly, but he didn't quite frown. "Let's hear what other ideas you gentlemen have in mind."

"A very attractive possibility is the Denver Federal Center," Sam Sloan said, doing a good job of hiding his relief. "Its location isn't as ideal as Kansas City's, it has to be admitted, but it's still fairly central. Also, it's quite handy to our friends in California."

MacGregor looked at him, his head cocked to one side. "As I remember, there's a certain small difficulty involving the Denver Federal Center," he said sardonically.

Sloan grinned. "You might say that."

"The Church of the New Dispensation's using the place for their western headquarters," McKay said. "Don't mean we might not be able to convince 'em to leave."

"I seem to recall they had a fairly substantial complement there," MacGregor said.

McKay shrugged massively. "Don't forget that a plague struck Denver right after the Freehold battle, sir," Sam Sloan said. "We know that caused them pretty disastrous losses. It may be that the DFC is not too strongly held."

MacGregor still looked skeptical. "Remember, we've got friends, like, not too far south from there," Casey Wilson put in. For once in his life McKay held back a smartass remark, out of deference to the President. Casey meant the Free-holders—and to him that meant raven-haired Angie Connoly, Dr. Marguerite's very own daughter.

"I don't know how reliable they'd be as allies," Sam Sloan said.

"They're hardly enthusiastic supporters of mine," Mac-Gregor said dryly.

McKay rubbed his jaw. "Anything to do with the New Dispensation bastards, they're with us."

"Finally," Sam Sloan said, "a California location offers a lot of enticement. Possibly in the LA area, possibly somewhere farther north. With the work New Eden and Dr. Morgenstern have done out there, we'd have ample resources to draw upon, and a fairly stable social structure over much of the area. Even with the devastation of the War and the trashing van Damm's terrorists did, there're excellent transport and communications facilities. And we do have a very active network in place that we can rely on totally."

MacGregor nodded thoughtfully. California had always been a major center of his support. "That does sound better. It sounds great, in fact."

McKay was looking sour. "It ain't all milk and honey," he said.

"What do you mean?"

"The FSE expeditionary force has gotten itself wedged in pretty tight out there. They even got New Eden. And they're liable to be a lot bigger pain in the ass than whatever's left of the New Dispensation in Denver."

MacGregor sipped his tea. "There's one more possibility that we ought to consider, gentlemen."

Eyebrows went up. "What's that, sir?" Tom Rogers asked.

"Washington, D.C."

For a moment silence filled the room like the sultry afternoon air. "Surely you can't be serious, Mr. President," Sam Sloan broke out. "Washington was subjected to intensive nuclear bombardment during the War."

"Wasn't all that intensive," McKay commented. "Parts of it were still standing when we left."

Sloan looked at him. "Surely you don't buy this—begging

your pardon, Mr. President, but this is a crazy scheme if I ever heard one.''

McKay shrugged again. "Okay. From a military point of view it sucks—sorry, Mr. President. But still, there's a part of me that says Washington is where we belong. It's the capital. It's a symbol, like. Something everyone can identify with.''

"Thus speaks the roughhewn philosopher,'' Sam Sloan said. McKay glared at him.

"Gentlemen, gentlemen,'' MacGregor said, making smoothing-down motions. "We shouldn't dispute among ourselves. I admit the idea of a return to Washington is a pretty farfetched notion. Still, it appeals to me—for just about the reasons Mr. McKay brought up.''

"I'm afraid it's out of the question, Mr. President,'' Tom Rogers said. "Half the city's rubbled out, and the rest is ruled by at least twenty rival gangs, from the information we've gotten out of there. It's a real madhouse.''

"I hear you, Tom.'' He sighed. "Then it looks as if there is just one choice remaining.''

"What's that, sir?'' Sam Sloan asked.

"Kansas City, of course. Just as I said at first.''

Sam Sloan found a well partied-out Billy McKay lying on the front glacis plate of the new Mobile One, his booted feet crossed, arms folded across his massive chest, his head resting against the bare metal of the turret just beneath the two gun muzzles. A fresh cigar was tipped to a real FDR angle.

"What's the matter, McKay?'' Sloan asked.

"Just enjoying the scenery.''

Sloan snorted. "Don't give me that, McKay. We've been together too long for you to fool me. Something's getting to you.''

McKay brought his eyebrows together like a pair of bleached caterpillars and hunched his shoulders. "Awright. I'm pissed off at the way Jeff turned pussy on us over this Mayor White thing.''

Sloan leaned on the vehicle. The foamed-alloy armor felt cool through the fabric of his coveralls. "I think he had a point, Billy. Dexter White's always been a good man. Don't forget he's the man on the spot; everyone in Kansas City has been looking to him for leadership and guidance since the War, and by and large he's pulled them through."

"Yeah. By makin' deals with them FSE cocksuckers."

"That's not true," said Sloan, exasperated. "Don't forget FSE had the authority of the last elected President of the United States to call upon—"

McKay looked away. "I ain't fucking likely ever to forget *that*." Not when he had personally fired the bullet that executed William Lowell.

The man was a traitor no matter how you cut it, the most highly placed traitor in the nation's history. By selling America to Maximov he betrayed everything McKay had ever stood for. And yet, he was the President, the man whose life McKay had once been sworn to protect at all costs. McKay wasn't a reflective man, but it was hard not to go through some pretty stiff changes over a thing like that.

Realizing what he had stumbled into, Sloan stuttered, "I—I—anyway, Mayor White had every reason in the world to believe it was perfectly legitimate to deal with FSE."

"He's a fucking rat bastard," McKay growled, "and you know it."

Sloan frowned. He could remember a time, not too long ago, when he'd looked in favor on the prospect that Dexter White of Missouri might become the first black president of the United States. "Come on, McKay, I think that's going a little far—"

"What about them scientists in Shawnee? He murdered them."

"That's not fair—"

"Fuck fair. He promised he would send in the cops and National Guard to put a cordon around that lab. He knew what would happen. Those goddamned New Dispensation maniacs just swarmed in and butchered them all. And he knew, Sloan. *He knew.*"

It was Sam's turn to look off, at the farmhouse with a few warm patches of lantern glow in the windows, the darkened town beyond, at the blunt thrust of Indian Knob dominating the town, at the starry sky, at nothing. He'd heard the last frantic broadcasts from the Oppenheimer Particle Accelerator

Facility, something over a year ago. Sloan's mind rebelled at the notion that it was Dexter White's intention. It just couldn't have been. Something had gone wrong. McKay should have known that; he understood the SNAFU principle as well as anyone. Maybe his anger was just latent racism coming out.

"Personally," McKay went on, as if to confirm Sloan's suspicion, "I'd like to put a bullet in that black bastard's ear."

Sloan shook his head ruefully. "Jesus Christ."

"What? So I'm a fucking racist? Is that what you're trying to tell me?"

Sloan bit his lip. "Yes."

McKay lifted his head and grinned at him. "Good," he said, "I'd hate to think I'm losing my touch." And he laid his head against the belly of the turret and went the hell to sleep.

CHAPTER
FIVE ——————————————————————

Another advantage Kansas City offered was that it wasn't too far from Heartland. Roughly three hundred fifty kilometers, south and west, brought you from Luxor, Iowa to Kansas City, Missouri. The Guardians set out in the morning of the day after the big party. Everybody was bleary-eyed from too much good time and too little rest. On the other hand, the celebration had really done something for each of them. It had been a welcome respite from the terror and violence of the previous forty-eight hours—and the seemingly endless months before.

Now they were bound back for the world. Or at least the world according to His Honor, Dexter White.

The convoy rolled out with the dawn, the newly christened Mobile One leading a liberated FSE expeditionary force truck carrying India Three and a load of fresh produce and other food, parting gifts of the townsfolk. Ranging before, behind, and to the sides like a pack of mangy wolves rode Dreadlock's Desperadoes. The residents of Luxor were a lot happier to see the last of them than to say good-bye to the Guardians; even though Dreadlock swore up and down that they had reformed and joined the ranks of the good guys, a lot of Callahan's crew had never quite shaken the time-honored outlaw biker addiction to outraging the citizens. Though no one's definition of a model of civic comportment, Dreadlock Callahan was nobody's fool. He'd done what he could to keep his scroungy troops in line. If they went too far they were certain to piss off the Guardians, and he knew what a poor idea *that* was.

Of course, being Dreadlock Callahan, the biker chieftain kicked over a few traces of his own. McKay was relieved, rolling south under a milky sky, that Mayor Jones hadn't found out just how friendly the outlaw had gotten with his baby sister.

Leavetaking had gone smoothly on the whole, and the Guardians had left behind several people they had felt unable or unwilling to keep with them. Quiet little Gillet—over whom Marla had even cried a little—and the skinny, blond-haired Sally. McKay just did not see himself carrying the President to safety with this freaked-out teenager hanging off his neck like an extra set of dogtags, and was glad he could leave the kid with Sally Ledoux. He also thanked God that he had convinced Dr. Marguerite Connoly to stay behind; he was still pissed at the way she had told him how to run her rescue.

They swung wide of Des Moines and then cut over to Interstate 35 and headed south. Soon they came into odd bumpy country, lush and green from hard summer rains. Little clapped-out towns lay scattered along their route like old cardboard boxes, long since depopulated by various of the Four Horsemen. After all this time, the decaying corpses of cars strung along most of the continent's roads had begun to look like just more natural features of the landscape.

The day got good and hot, under skies that went from milky to still-water blue, and then in the afternoon filmed over with gauzy high clouds that presently congealed into black-tipped thunderheads. The day before the war, Luxor to Kansas City would have been a reasonable day's drive. Now, with the roads unrepaired for over a year, scattered with the omnipresent wrecks, and the need to take it a little easy on vehicles that might be a spell before seeing replacement parts, the

Guardians planned to make the trip in two days.

With evening the sky exploded in three sudden purple-white flashes so intense everybody thought for one panicked heartbeat that somebody'd decided the U.S. hadn't gotten nuked enough in the One-Day War and decided to try again. It was only lightning, announcing the onset of a downpour that hit the turret topdeck of Mobile One like a mallet and bowed the truck's canvas back.

Billy McKay leaned over the wheel, trying to squint through the glass-and-plastic laminated-armor vision block. Even the wiper working overtime wasn't keeping it clear. "Get me a circuit to the troops," he told Tom Rogers, taking his turn in the ESO seat next to him. Rogers punched a button, nodded. "Callahan," he said into his throat mike.

" 'Drowned rat,' to my friends," came the laconic response.

"This shit's too much to drive through. See if you people can scout us out someplace decent to put up for the night. Preferably without occupants."

"With pleasure. Riding this weather is definitely not making any of us happy."

"Should have thought of that before you became an outlaw biker."

"Better watch the chatter, McKay," came Sloan's voice over the intercom. The ex-Navy man was up in the turret. "We don't want to pinpoint our location too exactly, just in case anybody's listening."

McKay made a face but decided not to say anything. His teammate was right. Having had a couple of days to pull themselves together, whatever FSE survivors were hanging around the hole where Heartland used to be might just about be thinking in terms of a little retribution.

A few minutes later Callahan came on the horn to report they'd found a little gas station a couple klicks ahead that seemed to have an intact roof and no obvious signs of occupancy. "There's even a little mobile home out back that would be a perfect nest for the lovebirds," the biker finished.

McKay chewed the stem of his cigar thoughtfully. "And just who the hell might you be referring to, Callahan?"

"Why, any young lovers who might feel that old spring sap running strong within them."

At McKay's side, Rogers chuckled. McKay jumped as if he'd just heard a round whang off Mobile One's steel side. Tom Rogers chuckled about as often as the Statue of Liberty. "Never knew you were such a poet, Dreadlock," the ex-Green Beanie said.

"For your information, Callahan, this is the twenty-first of fucking June, which is officially the first fucking day of summer," McKay said. "Spring's over."

He heard Dreadlock laugh. "It's the spirit of the thing that counts, McKay."

McKay coaxed the big car to a stop about five hundred meters from the gas station, next to a low hummock with a few dead trees on top. Small wonder the building seemed untenanted; this part of southwest Iowa lay smack in the middle of the rooster-tail of lethal fallout that swept down from Omaha, where the Strategic Air Command headquarters had been well plastered during the War. Fortunately, heavy-duty emitters decay fast; the vehicle's sensors were displaying readings only slightly higher than normal background radiation, so McKay wasn't worried.

In the old days, keeping watch while Callahan's men checked the building would have required popping the hatch and poking his crew-cut head out into the rain with a pair of binoculars hanging off his face. Now he just settled back in the special form-fitting swivel chair—like its predecessor this Mobile One was not your normal AFV—and punched a few buttons on the dashboard console. A computer-filtered TV picture of the view ahead appeared on a screen to the right of the vision block. McKay twiddled the controls some more until the pickup fixed on the front of the clapped-out gas station, where Callahan and four of his people had pulled up to a stop on the wet black asphalt. McKay brought up the magnification to show two of the bikers dismounting their cycles, one with a Remington 870 riot shotgun with a pistol grip and a silly-ass folding stock, the other with a stubby Colt Python, much like the one Sloan carried and McKay hated, but with a shorter barrel. McKay laced his stubby fingers behind his neck and grinned. "Ain't science wonderful," he said. "We got it all by remote control."

"We even have drones to do our housecleaning for us," remarked Sloan from the turret. He had his own screen up there next to his guns, which could be slaved to another screen or display input directly from the cameras on the hull.

While the guy with the pistol stood with his back against the wall, the riot gunner backed up to the door and kicked. Nothing happened; the glass had been blitzed, leaving a bare metal frame. Frowning through his thick beard, he bumped the center of the frame hard with his ass. And grimaced. The door was locked. In frustration he turned around, reached inside, fumbled briefly. Apparently he found the knob for the dead bolt, because the door finally yielded. He disappeared inside.

"Gee, Billy," Casey Wilson said. With something happening, he'd left the inflatable mattress aft of the turret root where he'd been sacked out since his duty turn to come and crane forward over Tom Rogers's shoulder. "It sure doesn't look like Dreadlock's people know too much about this sort of thing."

"They just ain't elite kill-trained commando types like us," McKay said. He unbuttoned a breast pocket of his coveralls, pulled out a well-chewed cigar stub, and stuck it in his face. His teammates would kill him if he lit it; at least it gave him something to chew on.

No sooner had he done so than the glassless door came banging open and the bearded biker in the sleeveless Levi's jacket came hurtling back out of the gas station. He appeared to have all these furry bags hanging off him. He stumbled at the run, sideways, batting at the things; fetched up against a gas pump standing askew where someone had put a fender into it, turned at bay. The shotgun was nowhere in evidence.

"Oh, wow," Casey said. "Those are dogs."

They sure as hell were. Half a dozen more came boiling out of the gas station, snarling and barking, lunging for the hapless biker as he batted at them with his hands. His buddy with the Python helpfully doubled over laughing. The other bikers, a woman and a sturdy Chicano, danced around waving their guns, afraid to shoot for fear of hitting their buddy.

His dreadlocks hanging as limp as well-boiled spaghetti around his shoulders, Callahan sat on his bike with arms folded across his chest and shook his head sadly. Tom Rogers cranked up the gain on the directional mike just in time to catch the words "You assholes are sure embarrassing the hell out of me."

"Shall I give him a hand, McKay?" Sloan asked. Through the hull they could hear him jacking open the breech of his M-203 grenade launcher—the one slung under his Galil. He was plainly intending to put a tear gas round into the homey little picture, but Callahan, as usual equal to the situation, was already helping himself. He leaned back and reached into one of the stained leather saddlebags hung on the rack over the rear tire. He came up with a grenade. He pulled the pin, leaned down, and rolled the can nonchalantly toward the snarling, cursing, twisting melee fifteen meters away. Then, still moving with steady lack of haste, he straightened up, pulled a well-soaked handkerchief from the breast pocket of his rain-damp coveralls, and pressed it fastidiously over his nose and mouth as the grenade bumped the curb next to a defunct soft-drink machine and began to spew great clouds of thick white smoke.

Dogs went in all directions. They came away from the hapless biker like bits of an exploding toupee, yipping in that broken shrill staccato dogs do when they hurt. The biker stood pawing at his eyes and cursing even louder. Their own eyes streaming sudden tears, the other bikers turned to swear at their leader.

"What are you so exercised about?" Callahan inquired unsympathetically, his voice muffled by the handkerchief. "Damn rain takes most of the sting out of that tear gas." It was perfectly true—but the peppery CS gas hit the dogs with their vastly more sensitive noses and mouths like a thunderbolt. Holding the kerchief over his mouth with his left hand, the biker leader pulled his big Redhawk out of his shoulder holster and started knocking over the running dogs, one after the other—pop-pop-pop—with single shots, as neatly as if they were beer bottles lined up on a rail fence.

"What's he doing," McKay asked, "busting caps to show off?"

"Don't want the dogs coming back to their den in the middle of the night," Rogers said.

Callahan donated another CS can to the worthy cause of clearing the rest of the pack out of the building. The other bikers, their eyes streaming tears, blasted the beasts as they came running out of the building. Then the convoy moved in to take possession.

CHAPTER
SIX ————————————————

Even with the vehicles parked outside, the little office next to the garage didn't offer a whole lot of room for everybody. Leaving a couple of bikers and protesting members of India Three on watch out in the rain, everybody moved inside to check out accommodations. What was offered was mostly cement floors with prehistoric grease stains smeared all over them. The place stank to begin with of decaying dog shit and piss and old meat; it quickly filled up with the additional odors of clothing soaked with grease, road grime, sweat, blood, and gun smoke and thoroughly wet down. Thankfully missing was that lingering sick-sweet smell of human flesh spoiling—once smelled, never forgotten—that always seemed to get into your clothes and your hair and the crevices of your body and stay like an unwanted relative. If there had been human carrion, the most recent occupants had disposed of it long since.

While a couple of bikers went around back to check out the trailer, Guardians medic Tom Rogers checked out the man who'd been jumped by the dog pack. His biker garb of denim and leather had protected him some from the ripping fangs of the animals, but not entirely; he had bad bites on his belly, calves and arms. Over his loud protests Tom Rogers cleaned out the wounds with disinfectant concentrate from the vehicle and shot him full of broad-spectrum antibiotic and a mono-clonal antibody for rabies. "This will make you as sick as a dog for at least twelve hours, son," Rogers remarked, not even aware of the pun. "Better find somebody to double up with tomorrow."

Jeff MacGregor came in, holding a liberated Austrian army jacket over his head to ward off the driving rain. "At least it's cool in here, if a bit humid," he said, after gagging briefly on the stench. The rest mostly took the smells in stride; they hadn't spent the time since the One-Day War in the climate-controlled confines of Heartland. He looked around.

A burly biker had settled himself in the office's one chair, a gray painted-metal contrivance with cracked green vinyl more or less holding together petrified foam padding. He had his scuffed black boots propped on the desk beneath a calendar bearing the faded image of a naked blond girl sitting on the seat of a tractor under a parasol, and even city boy Billy McKay knew no farm machinery like that had been vended in the United States of America since about 1957. His biker's belly, black furred with a graying band curving from the navel to disappear down into his tight leather trousers, was propped in his lap. "Let us borrow your chair, brother?" McKay asked. "I think old Jeff would like to sit in a chair that ain't moving for a while."

The biker cocked a shaggy eyebrow. "Who the fuck does he think he is?"

"The President of the United States."

"And who the fuck are *you*?"

With one hand Billy McKay grabbed the man's grease-soaked denim vest in the vicinity where his neck would have been if he'd had one. The other hand sank like a dagger into the bulge of fat and muscle above the skull belt buckle and grabbed a hunk. With a spasm of effort McKay powerlifted the biker up out of the chair, pivoted, and dropped him on the cement with a thump and a grunt and a clatter of assorted hardware.

"Billy McKay, asshole." He turned the chair around. "Have a seat, Mr. President?"

Looking faintly amused, MacGregor came forward and sat down. The other Guardians and Eklund's people were looking very wary as the burly biker picked himself up, spewing threats and curses and saliva. For all of Dreadlock Callahan's apparent friendliness, the alliance between soldiers and bikers was tenuous at best. But the other outlaws were all laughing at their comrade's misfortune.

The black-bearded man squared off facing McKay, who was ignoring him, studying the girl on the tractor. "Nobody does that to me and lives to tell about it."

"Then you've got nothing to worry about, *compadre*. Billy McKay ain't going to tell anybody about a little matter like this." It was Dreadlock Callahan, leaning against the door-jamb smoking his cigarillo. "Now quit fucking around with him, before he decides to mop up the garage with your face." The biker spat on the floor and banged through the glassless door into the rain. McKay and Callahan shared predators' grins.

Among the loot from the FSE convoy had been a neat little camp stove and cooking gear to replace India Three's, which was getting pretty tired. The Guardians had their freeze-dried rations for the microwave in the vehicle, but skinny little Cato, a white dude from the scratch platoon with lank black hair and vague eyes, had displayed a mastery of post-Holocaust cuisine of the funky but flavorful variety, so they were content to let him whip up something out of the foodstuffs they had brought from Luxor. They carried in a Telefunken multiband radio—more plunder—and set it up on an old workstand in the garage while Sloan and an electronically inclined biker rigged an antenna and began to fiddle with it. Meanwhile the work detail was clearing out some of the more unmentionable refuse. It was never going to be the Hyatt Regency, McKay figured, but it would probably do.

McKay got himself a bowl filled with Cato's goulash and chunk of bread baked fresh that morning. He settled himself next to the big German radio. "Getting anything interesting?"

"Well, expeditionary force traffic is still pretty hysterical, even in the clear." The recognition codes and scrambling routines for the whole FSE shooting match were already proving their worth. "We've got Casey monitoring the scrambled traffic outside. If anything interesting turns up, he'll let us know."

"What I want to know is what old Forrie has to say," Chi said around a mouthful of bread. His skinny black ass was propped on the rim of the saucerlike device used to mount and dismount tires from wheels. "I don't believe nothing until old Forrie tell me about it. He's got to be like Mr. Walter fucking Cronkite, man. Mr. News."

Cato gave him a twisted grin and turned the dial. "—cowardly terrorist attack," the all-too-familiar voice of Nathan Bedford Forrest Smith thundered from the radio. Not yet even thirty, Smith was one of the genuine powers remaining in the stricken North American continent. A former boy-wonder cable TV evangelist, Smith had built himself a citadel-cum-university deep in the heart of Oklahoma City, and settled back to await Armageddon, which a lifetime of fascination with doomsday prophecies had assured him was due along real soon now.

As it happened he'd been right. His reputation for infallibility had slipped somewhat, however, when shortly after the War he decided to back the charismatic and radiation-resistant prophet Josiah Coffin, becoming the first major convert to his Church of the New Dispensation. The destruction of Coffin and his crusading army by the Guardians and their allies in Colorado had left Smith at the head of a church badly wounded but still going strong.

He was today what he'd always been, a complete looney-tune who should have been the sort of excruciating embarrassment to the American Right that former California Lieutenant Governor Geoffrey van Damm—another party who, to his sorrow, had clashed with the Guardians—should have been to the Left. It was largely because numbers of people actually *listened* to nuts like those two that the country was as fucked up as it was right now, McKay privately believed.

Sandy held her hands over her ears, leaving her plastic ration tray teetering precariously on her knees. "Turn that *down!* It's jarring the fillings loose from my teeth."

"I've got to admit I'm rather interested in what Mr. Smith has to say," Jeff MacGregor said. "Do you think we could continue to listen at more moderate volume?"

Cato cranked the volume back down. "Okie City's not five hundred klicks away," Chi said. "You got fillings in you teeth, ought to pick them up anyhow."

After a barrage of lawsuits in the late 1980s, Smith's personal outlet KFSU had been the first radio station in North America to broadcast with a whole megawatt of power. It was hard to get away from the dulcet sound of Smith's voice, especially in Oklahoma City.

What Forrie Smith actually had to say was something of an anticlimax. He was denouncing a "terrorist" attack on an important but unnamed FSE installation in Iowa. He admitted it had caused heavy casualties—including the loss of at least one brigadier general—but letting out no more than that. Sam Sloan suggested that the expeditionary force was trying to break the news of Lowell's death and the destruction of its command structure slowly. But MacGregor said he thought it more likely Forrie in his outrage was spilling everything he knew. Nathan Bedford Forrest Smith wasn't the kind to make the most reticent ally.

Restless and irritable for no very good reason, McKay choked down the rest of his stew, stood up, and went out the back door. The rain had diminished. He stood there letting it bathe his face and soak his fatigues, staring blankly out across the pickup truck lying stripped in the yard among weeds, hood open and engine compartment gaping empty, doors gone, wheels gone, all fixtures even remotely movable gone, like some kind of freaky metal skull. Across the battered dumpster with the little elm tree shooting up to one side of it, already beginning to shift the battered metal box slightly with the inexorable pressure of growing. At the sorry mobile home, its windows broken, screens slashed, ancient cheap curtains faded almost to transparency flapping in the wet breeze. Out at the lumpy land of southwestern Iowa, impossibly green under the leaden sky.

He took a cigar from a breast pocket, cupped his hand over the end, and lit it with an electric lighter. He puffed it, took a deep breath. He liked the lush green and brown smells of the rain-wet land. But the cigar tang and hint of diesel fumes from out front lent a reassuring taste of his Pittsburgh home to the air.

He heard the metal knob turn in the door at his back. He didn't look around. A careful footstep, sound of the door closing, and lips lightly brushed the back of his bull neck.

He took the cigar from his face. "Either that's Sergeant Eklund," he growled, "or somebody's about to become KIA."

"You're a grouchy darned Yankee, ain't you?" He turned and grinned at the Texan drawl. He was still slightly taken aback at having a woman come so close to looking him straight in the eye. "Let's go check out that old trailer."

Though they were laagered down for the night, the Guardians had another, vitally important task to accomplish before they could sleep. But that was still several hours away. McKay shrugged and they started walking toward the trailer, the tall grass slapping wetly at their legs. The trailer was small enough to have its own wheels and not rest on some kind of built-up frame or foundation. A set of folding metal steps led up to the sprung screen door. The middle tread was missing.

McKay paused at the bottom. The place had a dead feel to it, and Callahan's bikers had supposedly given it a once-over. Nonetheless, he wasn't alive today because he took things for granted. He unsnapped the flap of the Kevlar field holster that carried his combat-modified .45. He noticed that Eklund had her hand resting as if casually on the butt of her Beretta service sidearm. "After you," he grunted.

Eklund grinned at him. When she grinned just that way, she had dimples. It went against everything Billy McKay had been brought up to believe in for a sergeant to have dimples. "Why, Ah do believe you might actually be turning into a gentleman."

She did a quick two-step up the stairs, moving very lightly for someone who weighed as much as a good-sized man. At the top she turned the flimsy little metal handle and opened the screen door. The inner door stood ajar. She started to push through.

McKay took his cigar out again. "Might be booby traps."

She turned and gave him the finger. "I'll make you pay for your Yankee perfidy, blue-belly."

McKay looked down. "My belly ain't blue," he said plaintively. She sniffed and went in.

Inside they poked around by the light of pocket flashes that could recharge off sunlight or plug into a car's dashboard lighter. The trailer had been pretty comprehensively trashed, naturally. McKay moved a dented aluminum coffeepot with bullet holes through both sides and waded toward the rear of the trailer through a mulch of papers and torn cloth that smelled heavily of mildew. "Somebody sure made a mess out of this place," Eklund said, shaking her head sadly. "They must have made off with everything that wasn't nailed down."

"Sonofabitch."

The sergeant looked sharply around. It was perhaps the first time in their acquaintance she'd ever actually heard Billy McKay sound surprised.

"Come here and take a look at this, will you?" McKay continued.

He was shining his flash into an open cubicle a little way toward the back and shaking his head heavily. "Will you look at this? They swiped the crapper. Somebody swiped the fucking *crapper*." His gruff, gravelly bass voice was outraged.

"I didn't think there was anything could shock you," Eklund said huskily.

He shook his head. "The crapper. Jeez Christ."

The trailer had a kitchen at the front, a little passageway past the cubicles that held the water tanks and bathroom, and a somewhat larger space in the rear that served as a combination living room and bedroom. That room was now bare except for the broken frame of what looked like the sort of cheap wooden chair once used to furnish efficiency apartments with. A little alcove to the left held a sofa bed, which was built into the trailer and couldn't be made off with. Eklund came up behind McKay and put a hand on his bare forearm. "Look at *that*," she purred. "Somebody's been mighty thoughtful."

Her fingertips seemed to brand his skin. He was suddenly acutely aware that he'd slept alone in Luxor. Spread out on the settee was what appeared to be a more or less brand-new sleeping bag, apparently, yes, *clean*.

He bent forward, sniffed. He normally wasn't exactly a fastidious type, but he did have certain standards, and these days you couldn't take anything for granted. "Clean," he said, half to himself. "What the fuck, over?"

He straightened and turned. Eklund already had her fatigue blouse half off. Her breasts were quite large, but showed no tendency to sag. Her nipples were pink, set in the midst of wide aureoles. Reflexively he reached out, cupped a tit in his big calloused hand, crushed the nipple with his thumb. It grew larger. Eklund bit her lip and growled deep in her throat.

McKay looked up at her. "Thought you were mad at me."

His hand started to pull away. Her hand shot out, caught the wrist, held it there. "I got over it. Just got to thinking . . ."

He looked at her.

"You're going to leave me—when this is over."

"Yeah."

"We won't know if we'll ever see each other again."

"True enough."

"Do you want to?"

"Probably."

The corner of her mouth quivered, curved up. "Thinking about it just put me off my feed for some reason." She leaned forward and kissed him. "Not that I think you're worth the bother."

He pulled her against him with his left arm. She flowed into him like warm water, her mouth covering his. Reaching blindly, he flipped back the corner of the old-fashioned zip-style sleeping bag. Something flat and rigid brushed his knuckles.

Still clinched with Eklund, he looked around. And stared. Resting there on the quilted fabric lining was a white business card engraved in gold. The cursive lettering read, *"With the compliments of Dreadlock Callahan."*

Lying next to it was a pack of Trojans.

CHAPTER
SEVEN ————————————————

"Guardians calling Mayor Dexter White. Guardians calling Mayor Dexter White."

Sitting in the ESO's seat with the hatch popped, Sam Sloan tipped his head back and watched the stars drift past overhead like schools of glowing tropical fish. It was an optical illusion, created by the motion of the patchy clouds. Somewhere up there, among those apparently moving schools of pinprick lights, was a smaller and nearer spark: a communications satellite, floating in geosynchronous orbit thirty thousand kilometers away.

The generation of satellites put into operation before the One-Day War had generally been of very self-contained designs: solar-powered, few moving parts, very ample computer memories so that they could suffer processing breakdowns, remap themselves, and commence functioning anew within a matter of hours. Many were still functional a year after the War. Heartland and the Guardians had made good use of them before, and the FSE invaders in their turn. Now the Guardians were putting DataStar 551 to use once again. The message was projected upward by a very small, low-power, computer-driven laser. The satellite beamed the message earthward—in theory, at any rate—at the Martin Luther King, Jr., Memorial Government Center in Kansas City, Mayor White's headquarters.

Of course, even the finest focus of the beam couldn't prevent the signal from blanketing an area of several square blocks. That was the reason for doing this now, in the dead of the night, when potentially prying ears would be at a minimum. They were sending on the mayor's special priority communications frequency. Some of his people were bound to be monitoring it, and not that many others. Unfortunately, among the others who were aware of the special channel were almost certainly whatever FSE troops were in town. That was the reason for all the precautions.

In the driver's seat next to him, Casey Wilson was slouched back with his head tipped well back, staring out his own open hatch at the night sky. He was wearing an AC/DC cap, as he didn't want to wear his treasured Springsteen 1975 "Born to Run" tour cap, which McKay had rescued from a doomed Heartland Complex, too much. Out of sight, sitting atop the silent turret, was the third member of the mini-expedition— Staff Sergeant Marla Eklund. She too was watching the sky, but a lot more intently than the two men. She was looking for FSE aircraft come searching for them, with a Stinger surface-to-air missile launcher all uncapped and primed and ready to go at her side.

The big armored car was parked on a hilltop fifty klicks east of the abandoned gas station. A derelict farmhouse, silent and eerie in the night, blocked the vehicle from view of the nearest road. Trees and outbuildings broke up the hilltop's silhouette, rendering the V-450 difficult to spot from air or ground. This was perhaps the trickiest phase of the whole operation. The Guardians were taking the fewest possible chances.

Fifty kilometers to the west, Rosie looked at Billy McKay and shook his head. "The way you staring at that thing, you gonna burn your eyes, man."

McKay didn't respond. Old campaigner that he was, he knew perfectly well that there was no way he could possibly see through the radio to what was happening fifty klicks away. He couldn't help himself. His two buddies—and Marla—were out there with their asses hanging in the proverbial breeze. And if things turned suddenly serious, there was nothing he could do to help.

The set-up had been laid to minimize the chance of detection, and to maximize the chance of successful escape if they *were* detected. Actually, at the moment Mobile One was considerably safer from potential snoops than the group clustered in the eerie bluish glow spilling from the verniers of the big German radio. Unless an airplane actually flew through the beam connecting the car with the DataStar satellite no one was going to pick up the outgoing transmission. And even the best radio direction finder gear couldn't detect a laser sender in operation.

Danger would start in earnest if and when Mobile One got a positive response to their feelers. If they did, they would put the mayor on hold, fire up the vehicle radio, and give a brief call to their comrades clustered in the gas station. That link, too, was as secure as it could be made: both stations were broadcasting a very directional, very low-power signal, and before leaving Sam Sloan had rigged the German radio to McKay's personal communicator, not only to boost the little pocket communicator's range, but so that the link between the camp and the vehicle could make use of the communicators' microminiaturized scramblers, so that any unwanted ears listening in on that leg of the conversation would hear only gibberish.

The problem was that RDF *could* detect both transmitters at that stage of the game if it was close enough, and otherwise could quite possibly pinpoint the location of one or both by simple triangulation. That was the chance that made McKay's palms so sweaty he was constantly rubbing them on his thighs, drying them unconsciously.

That and the necessity of splitting his team. It had happened before. During the fight with the New Dispensation and, more recently, during the run-in to the attack on Heartland, the Guardians found it necessary to divide their forces. But on a mission like this, conveying the President himself to a haven McKay personally didn't think was very safe, he did not like having the single organism which was the Guardians broken into lesser components. Likewise, sending a former cruiser officer and fighter pilot off on a delicate land mission still made him nervous, even though neither Wilson nor Sloan was a cherry in ground operations anymore. He would have preferred to have either himself or Rogers, past masters at land warfare, go along. But Sloan was the certified electronics whiz, and if trouble did break out nothing was more likely to get them out of it than the inspired lunacy of Casey Wilson's driving. Meanwhile there was still the President to think about. If by some chance the bad guys stumbled across the laager, McKay and Rogers were the maximum firefight men.

As for Marla . . . her second in command, the Kiowa corporal Tall Bear, could handle India Three's survivors if the whip came down, his wounds notwithstanding. And Eklund was the only non-Guardian whose proficiency McKay trusted enough to put on skysweep with the shoulder-fired SAM. As far as personal feelings were concerned—hell, he felt just a tiny smattering of guilt for not being *more* concerned. They were stuck smack in the middle of a mission and that was all he could really think about.

"McKay."

He picked up the little microphone jacked into the Telefunken. "McKay here. I read you."

"His Honor to speak to His Excellency."

Shit, McKay thought, *What am I? A fucking receptionist?* "You're on, Mr. President."

Jeff MacGregor nodded gravely to him. He took the microphone. "Dexter? This is Jeff MacGregor."

A pause, speckled with static. "Jeff? It's good to hear you." A dry hint of a chuckle. "Or should I call you 'Mr. President'?"

"That's affirmative." Traveling with the Guardians was giving MacGregor some bad speech habits.

"I confess I'm surprised at hearing from you. But pleasantly—pleasantly so."

"Dex, I have a very important favor to ask you. Not just on my behalf, but on behalf of the entire American people."

"Mr. President." The words were slow, low, mellow, and powerful. "I'm at your service."

They rolled down into Kansas City from the north, following

a route prearranged with Mayor White's liaison. The tenement streets of North Kansas City were mute and deserted under a cloud-filled sky. The growl of engines echoed hollowly off the soot-smudged brick faces of the buildings as Mobile One and the lone truck blitzed south, held above it all on the freeway's back.

"Just a few hundred meters to the bridge," Sam Sloan said. He was sitting in his usual position in the ESO seat peering through the vision block ahead of him.

"Too bad we don't have Callahan's people to scout ahead for us," Rogers remarked from the turret.

Hovering nervously behind Casey Wilson's right shoulder, Jeff MacGregor winced. "I understand how useful they could be for reconnaissance, and I am grateful for all the help they have given us. But I can't see Mayor White thanking us for bringing an army of . . . outlaw bikers into his city with us. This is a very delicate situation we have here."

"Besides," Sam Sloan said brightly, "there's nothing to worry about. Everything's all worked out."

Sitting in a fold-down seat to the rear of the vehicle with his legs stretched before him, McKay smiled grimly and said nothing.

The parting at a shopping mall outside the northern suburbs of Kansas City hadn't been particularly comfortable. "We're not exactly acceptable for your triumphal procession," Dreadlock Callahan had drawled around his narrow black cigarillo. "I can get behind that."

Standing with Billy McKay on the rain slick pavement beside Mobile One, wincing a little at the chill damp dawn breeze, Sam Sloan said, "It's not like that, Dreadlock. This is just a touchy situation. A lot depends on the initial impression we make on the locals. And you've got to admit, you've got a pretty rough-looking crew there."

Callahan tipped his head and cocked a sardonic eyebrow.

"Look, you've got to admit your people aren't the best disciplined in the whole wide world. They're good fighters, and they're smart, and we appreciate what they've done for us. But they're rowdy. And we can't afford the chance of them getting out of hand—can't afford any friction with the locals, whosever fault it is."

"Besides," said one of India Three's survivors behind him, "you've been paid."

The end of Callahan's mouth bent up. "Yeah. There is that."

"We don't want to go nowhere we ain't wanted," spat silver-haired Caprice. "Fuck 'em."

The other bikers growled ominous assent. Callahan waved a lazy hand in the air, cutting off their anger. "What must be, must be. See you boys around." And with that he brought his big Harley screeching around in a circle, pivoting on one jumpsuited leg, and led his Desperadoes screeching and wolf-calling off across the empty mall parking lot. One of them turned in the saddle to give the Guardians a final finger, and then they were gone.

"Shit," McKay had said.

Now Sam Sloan was feeling a little guilty about the ill feelings with which they parted. The Guardians owed Callahan and his people a lot. But Charles Ambrose, Mayor White's aide-de-camp, had spelled out in no uncertain terms that the President's welcome might be very strained if he turned up with a whole lot of mangy and heavily armed bikers riding in his entourage.

The reception committee was waiting for them as they approached the I-35 bridge across the Missouri River. There were a pair of white-and-blue police cars, a blue police van with wire mesh in the window glass and a squad of auxiliary officers in the back, and a yellow-tan official-looking sedan, all parked politely to one side of the southbound ramp.

As the convoy approached, the left rear door of the sedan opened and a man got out. He was wearing a white shirt, a dark tie, dark trousers that exposed an inch of white sock between pants legs and black shoes. His sandy hair was cropped fairly short, and his glasses had heavy black rims. The other rear door flew open, and a skinny kid of what looked to be college age scuttled around to open an umbrella over the jacketless man's head. At the same time, the door of one of the police cars opened, and a tall, lean, light-skinned black man in a navy blue suit with a moderate Afro also stepped out.

The convoy rolled to a halt with Mobile One's angular snout a discreet ten meters away. McKay crammed a steel-gray beret onto his short blond hair, opened the side hatch, and climbed down to the blacktop. As the three men approached he snapped off a salute of such perfection as to please even a Parris Island drill instructor—which made sense, since he'd *been* a Parris Island drill instructor. "William Kosciusko McKay, commanding the Guardians. Good morning, gentlemen."

The lanky black stopped and whipped off a very creditable salute in reply. *Military,* McKay thought. The blond man flogged the damp air once with his left hand. "Ambrose," he said in a dry, rather high-pitched voice McKay remembered from last night's radio conference. "This is Chief Peary of the city police." He adjusted the glasses on his pinched colorless face. "Is President MacGregor inside?"

McKay's outdoor tan whitened a touch at the corners of his mouth, but after a moment's hesitation he nodded crisply, turned, and held open the hatch. Ambrose pushed past into the vehicle without a word leaving McKay, Peary, and the flunky standing out on the pavement in the drifting mist. McKay stuck out his hand. Without hesitation, Peary took it, shook it with a firm grasp.

"This is a very great honor for the people of Kansas City, Lieutenant McKay." He sounded as if he meant it. McKay couldn't think of anything clever to say back, so he just shrugged. From over his right shoulder he heard Ambrose and MacGregor conversing in muted tones.

"So the expeditionary force people have really pulled out, huh?" he asked after a moment, looking the police chief right in the eye. Peary looked young to hold the job he had, not more than forty, forty-one. He looked very vaguely like a taller, tired Richard Pryor.

He nodded. "Not that there were that many left. We had as many as a thousand soldiers stationed here at one point in the early spring." Teeth showed beneath his mustache. "But they started having difficulties in various parts of the country. You folks wouldn't have had anything to do with that, now would you?"

McKay just grinned. "As of yesterday, there were no more than one hundred twenty-three FSE troops in the city. Mayor White requested that they withdraw, and they agreed to.

They'd pulled out by eighteen hundred."

"What did they have to say about it?"

"Colonel Derkszoon didn't seem very happy. But the troops were stationed here to help maintain order." Another smile. "My department has over a thousand men, including auxiliaries, and they're very well armed. They should be sufficient to keep order in Kansas City, don't you think, Guardian McKay?"

Obviously this Chief Peary had taken no little pleasure from facing down the FSE Colonel What's-his-name. If he were telling the truth, that is—and McKay had a gut feel that he was. He was frankly surprised. On the other hand, Dexter White had gone along with the idea of breaking with the FSE and declaring for MacGregor with virtually no argument at all. Perhaps he sensed the expeditionary force's days were numbered and wanted to be sure he was in with the winner. *Or maybe I been misjudgin' him all along.*

Ambrose's sandy head stuck out of the hatchway. "We are ready to proceed, gentlemen. Ben, you may ride back with the car."

The flunky obediently walked off toward the official-looking sedan. Ambrose disappeared back into Mobile One. McKay nodded to Peary. "Good to meet you."

"Pleasure."

McKay waved back to Marla Eklund, sitting in the passenger seat of the truck directly behind the V-450. Then he climbed into the vehicle and slammed the door.

CHAPTER
EIGHT ────────────────

Chief Peary's police car pulled out onto the ramp and kicked in its blue flashers, but no siren. He had no intention of trying to put himself ahead of the President in any figurative way. He was simply putting his car in the lead so that the sight of a strange armored car rumbling through Kansas City streets wouldn't freak out the inhabitants too much.

Dreadlock Callahan's comment notwithstanding, this was not meant to be a triumphal entry. It had been agreed to defer announcement of Jeff MacGregor's resumption of the presidency until he was well ensconced in King Memorial Center and had at least one face-to-face meeting with Dexter White and his advisors.

Casey let in the clutch and followed the chief, Sam Sloan casting warning glances sideways at him to warn him not to tailgate. Casey was a Grand Prix–level driver, but tended to get overenthusiastic. The city car and the other cruiser waited patiently until Mobile One and the truck had rumbled past, then Ambrose's car swung into line with the last blue-and-white, its light bar flashing, bringing up the rear.

Swollen by rain, the Missouri showed frothy white-capped bands drifting along its surface like interference patterns scanning across a TV screen. To Sam Sloan's eye it was apparent that only the substantial cement levees had kept if from flooding the city's center. Even they weren't invariably effective; way off to the east he could make out the tiny vigorous shapes of what looked suspiciously like a sandbagging crew.

Somewhere deep inside, part of him relaxed. Sloan was an old Missouri boy himself—not from around here, but from the southern part of the state, the green heights of the Ozark Plateau. Still, this was homecoming in a sense, and it felt good.

Ambrose occupied the fold-down seat behind Casey Wilson, directly opposite MacGregor. McKay took his customary seat in the back. "I didn't see too many signs of life in the part of town we've just been through," the President said.

Ambrose's black eyes—startling in such a fair-skinned face—roved the cabin like small inquisitive animals, probing every nook and cranny. They darted back to MacGregor. "We found it necessary to evacuate the suburbs in the north city," he said. "We thought it would be expedient to have our population as centralized as possible."

"Where you can keep an eye on them, huh?" Billy McKay grunted.

Ambrose stared at him. "Excuse me?" he almost barked, in a *"Did you fart, or what?"* tone of voice that told McKay the comment had been unappreciated, and so would anything else he might care to say. McKay's jaw set very tight and a vein began to throb at his left temple. Sam Sloan cast him a pleading look over his shoulder.

In the normal course of events, McKay would have picked the likes of Mr. Charles fucking Ambrose up by both ends, twisted him, and wrung all the juice out of him like a slimy bar rag. That was not going to do much to win the hearts and minds of the population of the nation's new capital. Besides, he realized he really had spoken out of line. He was just a grunt, and had no damn business pushing his face in when the President was involved in serious talk. He shook his head. "Sorry."

They rumbled south, downtown. Past a big expanse of astonishingly well kept trees and grass on the left-hand side the freeway veered west. The police car led them on a way, off a ramp with a sign above it that had been blistered into illegibility by the one-megaton blast that had taken out the eastern suburb of Independence. Downtown was the standard rock garden of glass boxes of various dimensions. What made them unusual was that few of them had any glass at all on their eastern faces. Sloan noted a lot of the broken windows had been planked over with plywood sheet or scraps of wallboard on lower floors.

There were people on the streets, more than the Guardians were used to seeing, but somehow not as many as Sam Sloan expected. There was something about the way they moved. . . . Not that they moved with the furtive scurry of rats invading a pantry, as did the denizens of the really wild rubbled-out zones. Neither did they walk head up and without a care in the world like the people of Luxor, Iowa. They went about their business upright, but there was a certain rapid, almost jerky quality to their movements, and their heads seemed to swivel incessantly on their necks like radar antennas. The reaction to Mobile One itself bothered him, somehow. People would snap around, stare at it hard, and then look elsewhere. *Anywhere* else.

He could imagine the dilemma Mayor White had found himself in. He knew White was a good man, a marrow-convinced liberal. He couldn't have welcomed the intrusion of the FSE troops. At the same time, White had a rep as a very pragmatic man; he had to know what would happen if there were any incidents between his townspeople and their "protectors." So he'd probably found himself in the ugly position of having to lean hard on his own people, much harder than he thought fair. For their own good. The last few months had been tough on the people of Kansas City, Sloan guessed. And toughest of all on Dexter White.

Their odd procession comprised the only cars on the street. The pedestrians seemed to be mostly going about their business, walking on the sidewalks, pushing improvised carts, going in and out of shops along either side of the street. Those with an eastern exposure tended to have their window glass replaced by wallboard or whatever, as Sloan had already noticed, and a good many of them here were painted with varying degrees of expertise, from a series of spray-painted birds and faces that looked as if they had been done by a not particularly talented third-grader to a mock Maxfield Parrish air-brushed landscape of a mountain lake with distant snow-covered peak reflected in it. Had Sam Sloan been beholding this scene in any American city say, two years earlier, he'd have felt as if he'd fallen into the Twilight Zone. But now the whole scene had such an air of normality—compared to what he had grown used to in the past year—that it almost brought tears to his eyes.

They turned a corner and there was the Martin Luther King, Jr., Memorial Government Center, built after the riots of the early 1990s gutted most of downtown Kansas City. It was a huge compound, covering several hectares; a gleaming white structure five stories tall, built in the shape of a U facing north towards the riverfront and enclosing a flagstone plaza complete with fountain—which, to Sloan's amazement, was running, water shooting up a good five meters in the air in the midst of an oblong pool. The bottom floor was a sort of arcade, interstices filled in with dark polarized glass. Two stories above that were faced in gleaming white cement panels figured with huge X's like expressed structural struts. The top two stories were courses of more polarized-glass windows.

"The windmill's running." Sitting in the back, McKay cocked an eyebrow. It had been Sloan's voice. He looked forward, but Ambrose and the President had their heads together and didn't appear to have noticed the comment. Apparently Sloan had subvocalized it in his throat mike and piped it through the vehicle's intercom system to McKay's earplug.

"Yeah, I see that," Casey said in the same way. "Like, what's so special about that?"

"I remember it caused a big hooray when they opened this place a couple of years ago. The wind-power generator made so much noise the citizens complained. Mayor White finally had to close it down." Rebuilding the heart of Kansas City had been a major part of Mayor White's electoral platform. The new Center had been built to his specifications as the nerve center for a vital, aggressive, progressive city government. One of its better-known features was that it was built to provide more space than the current city administration needed, the implication being that with the popular mandate White would soon expand operations to fill available space. And even in the diminished-expectation days of the early nineties his charisma had been enough to carry it off.

Another feature of the complex was that it was designed to take maximum advantage of alternative energy sources—notably solar and wind power. Craning his neck to squint through the view slits, McKay could see that the roof was topped with arrays of solar panels like south-facing bleachers, their benches replaced by mirrors. High up on a mast of tubular metal struts, the fifteen-meter mill of a wind-power generator turned slowly in the damp and desultory morning breeze. It represented, so Sam said, Mayor White's first—and as of the One-Day War only—defeat of note. The damn thing apparently made a noise like the Tin Woodman being flayed alive, an absolutely ungodly metallic screeching and banging and moaning. It had elicited complaints first from what businesses remained in downtown Kansas City, which White shrugged off; subsequent complaints from the predominantly black Downtown Neighborhood Association were rather harder to field. At first White's office tried to discredit the leaders of the petition drive as politically motivated, but a suit in Federal Court and close scrutiny from the Environmental Protection Agency forced him to back down. The windmill had been shut down.

Now Mayor White was undisputed boss of Kansas City, and it was back on again.

At Ambrose's direction Mobile One turned to drive along the open mouth of the U. Across the street rose a six-story open parking structure, dark tiers alternating with ruddy brown bands of masonry. "You can turn your vehicle in here, Lieutenant," Ambrose said, indicating the garage. "Park on the ground floor. I don't think the higher levels will support the car's weight."

"Negative," McKay said. Ambrose and MacGregor looked at him, the President blankly, the other one blinking hostilely behind the thick lenses of this glasses. "Turn left here, Case."

"Right up onto the plaza?"

"You got that right."

"Now, just a minute here!" Ambrose exclaimed. "You just

can't go driving across there. It will break all the paving—''

"Billy, we need these people's friendship," MacGregor said quietly. McKay stuck out his jaw. "This is an unsecured area, Mr. President. And as long as I'm in charge of your safety, you're not walking across the street in front of God and everybody in the middle of what was enemy territory until only a few hours ago.''

To punctuate his argument Casey cranked the wheel obediently left. With a thump and a crunch the big V-450 climbed the curb and rolled toward the building. The occupants could hear the dull crackling of cement fracturing beneath the tires. "Anyplace in particular you'd like me to park her?'' Case Wilson asked cheerfully.

"We've been planning to accommodate you in the right wing of the complex, Mr. President,'' Ambrose said after a moment's glare at McKay. "The mayor's offices are in the left wing. He's looking forward to receiving you as soon as is, ah, convenient.''

"Park right over here on the right up against the building, then, Casey,'' McKay instructed. "We can walk around on the inside.''

"If you aren't afraid someone will bushwack you in the corridors,'' Ambrose blurted.

McKay unclipped his M-60E3 Maremont lightweight machine gun from the clips that held it to the hull. "Anybody does that,'' he said snapping open the feed tray and slamming down the first cartridge of a belt protruding from the half-moon Aussie ammo box, "we'll just have to take care of 'em, won't we?''

He stepped out first. Muggy heat hit him in the face like a wet blanket; it was shaping up to be a hell of a hot day. The driver of Marla Eklund's truck had followed up on the plaza, leaving their official escort floundering around out on the street. McKay waved to the truck to park behind Mobile One.

The passenger door opened. Eklund popped down onto the red pavement, walked forward, gave McKay a quick squeeze on the arm. "Go get some people to show you where we are going to be hunkering down. You get your personnel settled in while we go meet Hizzoner,'' he told her.

Ambrose's bespectacled head poked out of the open hatch.

"We've made arrangements to accommodate your . . . friends
. . . in a dormitory a few blocks from here—"

"No way. They're sticking with us until we make damn
good and sure things have shaken out right."

Ambrose hopped out of the vehicle and stood glaring up at
McKay. He looked like a terrier trying to stare down a bull-
dog. "Your attitude is insufferable! You come rolling in here
in your gigantic war machine, you start passing out orders and
dictating to everyone as if you're, you're—"

"The President of the United States." McKay nodded at the
open door. "That's him, right there. And we're his body-
guards."

MacGregor stood looking glumly down at the pair. "Lieutenant McKay, I appreciate your solicitude. But please, can't
you go easier on Mr. Ambrose? He's only trying to make the
best of a difficult situation." Ambrose gave McKay a shit-
eating smirk and nodded. Restraining the urge to smash his
face for him, McKay shrugged.

"Casey, you stay with the vehicle. Tom, go inside and help
Sergeant Eklund get her people settled in. Sam, come with me.
We're going to take a little walk."

The reception committee had been all set to receive the
President and his entourage in the other wing of the building,
a hundred meters away across the plaza. A call over Mobile
One's radio brought several people scurrying over to show
Tom Rogers and India Three the area set aside for their use.
While they were waiting, Chief Peary left his cruiser parked at
the curb and came strolling up with his hands in the pockets of
his trousers. He looked Mobile One over carefully before saying, "I can see I'm going to have to give you fellas a lecture on
the parking laws in Kansas City."

McKay grinned at him. There was somebody in KC he could
like, at any rate.

The guides arrived and India Three deassed their truck.
They stood rubbernecking around at the big gleaming white
complex making wondering comments, their packs and weapons slung over their backs. A short, trim young woman with
an outdoor tan and curly black hair walked up to the group
standing beside the V-450. She had on jeans and a white
blouse, work boots, a very bright smile. "Good morning, Mr.

Ambrose. And you must be President MacGregor?" Mac-
Gregor smiled, nodded, extended his hand. She shook it. "I'm
pleased to meet you, sir. Please excuse the informality but we
weren't, uh, prepared for you to arrive here." A quick glance
at Ambrose. "And you gentlemen must be the Guardians."

Sam Sloan grinned his best folksy aw-shucks grin. "That's
right, Ms. This is William McKay and I'm Sam Sloan. And
you are—"

"Oh, just call me Chris. Like I said, we're not big on for-
mality. Shall we go? Mayor White is dying to meet you."

She glanced back across the open plaza. Feeling Ambrose's
eyes on him, McKay nodded heavily toward the gleaming glass
door. "This way, if you don't mind." Since he'd played his
presidential security card, he wasn't about to back down by
letting MacGregor walk across a football field's worth of open
air. And he wasn't just playing macho games with Ambrose;
there were a *lot* of windows in this damn complex. And it
would just take one man with one rifle behind one of them.

With a shrug Chris led them inside. The air was still and
stale. "Please forgive the way it is in here," she said. "We
shut down the air conditioning after the FSE troop with-
drew."

Sloan raised an eyebrow. "Air conditioning?" Mayor
White had been a vocal supporter of appropriate technology,
and had frequently criticized Western man's habit of shielding
himself at all costs from the vagaries of the natural environ-
ment.

Ambrose glared at him poisonously. Chris dropped her eyes,
embarrassed. "Yes, it seems a little inappropriate, doesn't
it? Especially since we have to run special generators we've
converted to alcohol to keep the ventilation system going.
But, you see, there aren't any windows."

"No windows?" McKay frowned, gestured at the continu-
ous sheet of rippling polarized glass that formed the left-hand
wall of the corridor they were walking. "What's all this?"

"They don't open, McKay," Sam Sloan said. "These are
modern buildings."

"Mayor White was furious. He tried so hard to make sure
every detail of the new center was perfect. But there's only so

much one man can do—'' An aggressive throat-clearing from Ambrose cut her off.

"And what's this?'' McKay said, glancing upward as they passed through a doorway in what looked like a structural wall. There was a slot cut overhead in the dropped tile of the ceiling.

"Oh that? You're not really supposed to see that.''

"Those are fire-containment panels,'' Ambrose said stiffly.

"Oh, they do more than that. Everyone was very uptight about terrorism when this place was designed. At the press of a button, these bulletproof Plexiglas panels slide down out of the ceilings to cut off access among the three segments of the Center.''

Ambrose looked daggers at her. "Really, there's no need to burden our guests with irrelevant details of the Center's construction.''

Sloan smiled encouragingly at the woman. "Oh, we don't mind.''

"Yeah,'' McKay grunted. "We got a President to look after, after all.''

As they passed through the central section of the complex, they began to see people conducting their daily affairs, working by dim photocell-generated light in offices adjoining the walkway, hurrying down the corridor, sparing a quick glance at the curious procession before moving on.

The center of this section was given over to a wide, tall, echoing hall, with the seals of state and city inlaid in the floor. Ground level was taken up by little cubbyhole offices, information kiosks, a tiny newsstand. As they passed Sam Sloan grinned, half-saddened, half-humored at seeing the cover of *Vogue* with Hollywood siren Merith Tobias modeling the latest swimwear and the last-ever issue of *Time* magazine featuring the grizzled, lynx-eyed visage of Soviet Premier Butenko. They seemed to belong to another time . . . another generation. Another planet, perhaps. An old black man in stained tan coveralls was mopping the great seal of the State of Missouri with water from an old galvanized metal bucket on wheels with the wringer attached to one side. He was whistling to himself. He didn't look up as Sam Sloan glanced his way;

and the others didn't even notice him.

As they approached the Mayor's sanctum, the complex started showing progressively more signs of life. It was as if the people of White's administration had wanted to keep as much distance as possible between themselves and their FSE "friends." Swinging along at Sam's side, Chris said, "You seem surprised there aren't more people here."

Up front, Ambrose and MacGregor had their heads together again. *Probably trying to smooth over McKay's breaches of etiquette,* he thought. He had tremendous respect for the leader of his team, but there were times when Billy McKay's blunt manner—and overly suspicious nature—proved a positive embarrassment.

"This is the administrative center for what may be the most populous city remaining on the North American continent," he said. "Somehow I expected to see a few more people."

She looked away quickly. "Mayor White believes in an activist administration. Most of our personnel are out working among the people." She looked back. A glint of teeth showed white against her smooth tan face. "I'll take you out tomorrow, if you like, show you what we've accomplished." He could feel pride and enthusiasm beating off her like heat from a stove.

"If you ain't too busy chasing tail," a voice whispered in his ear, "you might take note of how many uniforms with guns just happen to be drifting around this part of the world." He blinked; it was McKay, subvocalizing so that his teammates would hear him through the bone-conduction phones behind their ears without anyone else in the party being aware he'd spoken.

"Ease off, McKay," he returned in the same manner. "We're among friends."

"If you say so."

Once in the easternmost leg of the U Chris steered them toward a bank of elevators. A pair of city police guards with billed caps and sidearms and shiny Sam Browne holsters were holding one just for them. Sloan cocked an eyebrow as the door shut and the elevator began to whisper upward. "You don't expect to make the President walk up five flights of stairs, do you?'' Chris stage-whispered to him. Ambrose shot her a thin-eyed glance. Even diplomat Sam was beginning to find him difficult to take.

At the top there were two more KC cops waiting for them with smiles and nods. Like the ones downstairs, they were armed only with sidearms and mace canisters at their belts. Down among his bones McKay knew there were going to be some better armed troopies, possibly decked out in body armor, hanging around somewhere out of sight. For a beloved leader of his community, Dexter White didn't seem to believe in taking too many chances where his personal safety was concerned.

They were in an interior corridor. Sunlight spilled in through expansive skylights overhead, touching the off-white walls and the paisley carpet with a mellow morning glow. Potted plants waved fronds and leafy branches in the slightly astringent artificial breeze. Charles Ambrose cleared his throat, straightened his back and his tie, and stepped out with wide toe-reaching steps to lead the way. It was obviously all Chris could do to keep from skipping ahead; she seemed too thrilled for words by the impending meeting between her beloved boss and the President of the United States.

Without conscious thought McKay and Sloan took up position on MacGregor's right and left. MacGregor glanced both ways, smiled a private smile. He was safe here, he knew. Nonetheless, it was good to know he had men such as these to back him up.

A black policewoman and a mustachioed male cop of Oriental descent stood guard over the open doorway to Mayor White's reception room. They saluted crisply. McKay and Sloan once more slapped off parade ground responses; MacGregor smiled and sketched a salute of his own. They passed into a spacious anteroom so dominated by exotic overgrown plants that McKay almost wished for a machete. From behind a desk tucked discreetly away to the left a youngish man with pale blond hair wheeled himself out to greet them; both his legs had been amputated several centimeters above the knees.

"Gentlemen," he greeted them. He rolled the wheelchair to the gleaming oaken door to the office, rapped with his knuckles. "Mr. Mayor, the President is here."

Charles Ambrose stepped briskly forward and held open the door. Inside, across an expanse of dark green rug large enough to land a chopper, at a desk you could park Mobile One on, Mayor Dexter White of Kansas City, Missouri, was rising to greet his visitors.

CHAPTER
NINE ————————————

McKay wanted to hate him.

It had started over a year ago. The Guardians came to Kansas City when lingering radiation from fallout was still at redline across much of the United States—indeed, much of the world. It was the first stop in their quest for the scientists and experts who made up the mysterious Blueprint for Renewal. They were looking for one Dr. James Okeda, a researcher at the Oppenheimer Particle Research Facility in the suburb of Shawnee, across the Kansas line.

Speaking with McKay in person over the city's cellular telephone system, Mayor White had welcomed him and his team, offered them every assistance. Yet somehow it hadn't seemed to work out that way. When they hit Shawnee they found the Oppenheimer facility surrounded by a fanatical mob of what proved to be followers of the Reverend Josiah Coffin, First Prophet of the Church of the New Dispensation. The First Prophet's message had a very chameleonlike habit of adapting itself to whatever background it was laid against; the colors it wore for this crowd ran to antitechnology and blood in the streets.

It had been a brutal awakening for the Guardians, even

though each of them was seasoned in the brutalities of modern warfare. In spite of the undisputed control he held over most of the city, Dexter White was doing nothing to contain the mob. The Guardians had to fight their way into the labs and out again—and a sniper robbed them of Okeda, the prize they had come to gain.

With time pressing in on them—every day's, every hour's delay in reassembling the Blueprint cost American lives—the Guardians couldn't hang around to protect the peaceful scientists at the facility. Ever helpful, Mayor White offered to extend full police protection to the besieged researchers. The Guardians took their leave and headed for Colorado to follow their next Blueprint lead.

Some hours later, they got a frantic call from Oppenheimer saying that the mob was coming over the wire—*and Mayor White had withdrawn his police cordon*. Then silence. A silence you heard ringing in time with the pulse across your eardrums late at night when you couldn't sleep.

McKay wanted to hate Mayor White. But he could tell right away it was going to be hard.

He was a big man, maybe just a centimeter or two shorter than McKay himself. He was large-framed and not exactly emaciated in a navy blue suit with only the subtlest pinstriping; by his looks he'd never been athletic, but neither was he particularly soft. He had a large rather prematurely balding head, fringed by thick black wiry hair, dusted with gray at the temples. "Mr. President," he said somberly, "In the name of the people of Kansas City, I welcome you."

MacGregor stopped a few meters away. "Thank you, Mr. Mayor. It's both an honor and a pleasure to be here. I'm confident that our association will be both long and productive for the people of the United States of America."

Dexter walked a little stiffly—more like a man who has a bad back than a pompous one, to McKay's eye—around the edge of the desk. Then he broke into a huge grin that accented the apple roundness of his cheeks, and his eyes almost vanished into laugh lines behind the tinted lenses of his streamlined glasses.

"Jeff!" he exclaimed, taking three quick steps forward to

grab the President by the upper arms. "It's great to see you, man."

MacGregor grinned back and slapped him on the back. *I can almost hear the shutters clicking,* McKay thought.

"And these gentlemen must be—?"

"The Guardians," MacGregor said. "Dexter, let me introduce Commander Sam Sloan and Lieutenant William McKay."

White stepped forward. "A pleasure to meet you, gentlemen. A very great pleasure indeed."

Sam took the proffered hand. "It's my pleasure, Mr. Mayor. I've admired your work for many years."

"Why, thank you, Commander," White said with what seemed genuine pleasure. It appeared to fade somewhat as he turned to McKay. "Ah, Lieutenant McKay. It's a . . . pleasure . . . finally to encounter you in the flesh." The Mayor's last conversation with McKay—a year ago—had not ended on a friendly note.

McKay took his hand. For a moment he thought about putting a real drillpress crunch on the man. He felt Sloan's and MacGregor's eyes on him. *Hearts and minds, Billy,* he thought, *hearts and minds.* He forced himself to grip the hand firmly and no more. The answering clasp was just as firm and seemed as precisely measured. *Maybe there's more to this dude than I think.*

"Charles, Chris, good to see you. Gerald, will you have refreshments brought in for our distinguished visitors?" The receptionist in the wheelchair nodded from the doorway and turned away to his desk. MacGregor settled himself in a leather-covered chair set off to their left, facing the mayor's desk. The others followed his example, taking chairs placed behind his.

White sat with his back toward a glass wall that looked out over downtown Kansas City. Through the window the city presented an eerie appearance of *everyday*—the boarded, decorated window covers mostly out of sight on the ground floor, the blank eastern faces of most buildings giving somehow the appearance that they still had windows that didn't happen to be reflecting light at this time of day. The city appeared as it might have on any half-overcast morning before the One-Day

War. Until you noticed that there were no cars moving in the streets, few people. Few signs of any kind of life.

It hit Sloan hard. *And this is one of the lucky places,* he thought.

The wall to their right was dark wood paneling, covered with photographs of Dexter White at various periods of his career: Mayor White with Jesse Jackson; greeting foreign dignitaries; assuming the chair of the Black Mayors' Caucus—a position he held when the War came down; a gangly, bespectacled White in his teens with painfully short hair and prominent ears meeting the Reverend Martin Luther King, Jr. A picture of Dexter White at a thousand-dollar-a-plate fundraiser, shaking hands with none other than Jeffrey MacGregor.

A young man dressed in jeans and polo shirt pushed in a refreshment tray. White and MacGregor chose orange juice, Sam Sloan coffee; ignoring Ambrose's pinch-faced look of disgust, McKay asked for a beer, and was handed a chilled, if aged, can of Bud.

White and MacGregor were talking earnestly of all the great things they were going to do for Kansas City, the United States, and the world. Great. It was none of Bill McKay's business and, frankly, bored the snot out of him. But his years of service in the Marine Corp served him well; like an old campaigner, he pulled himself upright in the chair, propped his eyelids wide open, and went straight to sleep.

The rest of the day was given over to discussions between MacGregor and White and his city administration. When a lunch break was finally called, McKay woke up, excused himself, and got on the horn for Casey to come take over for him while he returned to the bivouac area to shake it down for security and get it ready for occupancy. Casey was a lot better socialized then he was; he could make the appropriate nice noises.

Ambrose protested that there was no need for McKay to bother; the Mayor's security people had the situation well in hand. McKay fixed him with a stare the color of the sky over tundra. "I'm chief officer in charge of presidential security. And until I'm satisfied that the President's security is absolutely assured, he's going to have at least two Guardians with him at all times." He paused a moment. "Not that I'm running down your security arrangements or nothing, Mr. Mayor." Sam Sloan rolled his eyes heavenward. McKay nodded and went out.

He backtracked the route they'd taken here. He really wanted to wander around a bit farther afield and get a better feel of the place, but there was only so far even he'd push his luck. He'd taken in all the details already, but he checked them over again for thoroughness' sake. Let Jeff and Sam go on thinking everything was fine. He was looking for the whip to come down. And besides, he never liked to slack off in the field.

As he ambled along he hauled out a cigar and stoked up. Immediately a middle-aged woman in a brown skirt and black stockings popped out of some cubicle and stabbed a forefinger at a sign that showed a smoking cigarette with that international slash-in-circle symbol stamped on it. He nodded politely and walked on, wondering, *What the fuck's eatin' her? I ain't smokin' no cigarette.*

Tall Bear met him on ground level back in their wing with a grunt, and an upward nod when he asked where the sergeant was. Tall Bear was never gonna be a fan of his, he could tell. It didn't bother him. No ex-DI really cares if he's loved, so long as the people around him pull their weight. Tall Bear did; that ended it.

He climbed a flight of stairs to find Rogers sitting behind a receptionist's desk leafing through a thick sheaf of printout. "How does it look?"

"Didn't actually quarter the troops here. Just the officers." That fit McKay's image of the Effsees. "There are some real-live apartments up on five. Lived there, otherwise used the place for admin and HQ."

"Where we gonna sleep?"

It went without saying that MacGregor would get the dedicated living quarters. "There's room. Lounges on every floor with sofas in 'em. Lots of carpet."

McKay nodded. "Where's Eklund?"

"Few doors down. Got a little commissary; stocked pretty good, she says."

"Effsees know how to live right, and they got the guns to

make it happen. What you reading, anyway?"

"Printout of post returns." The daily record of personnel status, who was on leave, on sick call, or in the slammer. Not the highest-drawer security, but not necessarily something you left lying around for the enemy to read. McKay shrugged, moved on.

Marla was sitting with her ass propped on a stainless steel counter next to a coffee urn, sipping hot chocolate from a foam cup. She nodded to him. "Put that danged rope out if you plan to come in here, Yankee. You want to stink the place up to high heaven?"

"Speaking of that, you need to see about rigging showers for your people. They smell like wet fucking dogs."

"Two nights in that old gas station, what did you expect?" Sip. "They got showers, anyway. Hot water, even; thought I'd died and gone to heaven when I tried turnin' it on and it came out steamin'. I was waiting for you to get back an' okay our arrangements before I sent 'em off to scrub up."

"Great. How're you set?"

"We don't have a whole lot of people. Decided to put 'em all on the floor under Mr. MacGregor's. Maybe have a pair patrolling the stairwells all the time."

"You don't trust this arrangement either, huh?"

A shrug. "Don't have no feelin's one way or t'other. You asked me to set up secure. I did."

He nodded. He still felt weird, holding a straight-out military conference with a woman he'd screwed, but he wasn't going to let it get to him. "Like you to do something else before your people shower. I want to test your walkie-talkies, make sure the structural beams in the building don't fuck up point-to-point transmission inside. And I'll want your people to unload some stuff from Mobile One."

She tossed the cup into a gray plastic can with a petrified green plastic liner inside, straightened. "I'll get Jim to run the tests. When do you want to offload the gear?"

"In a bit. Something I have to do in the car first."

She waited for an explanation. After a moment she sighed. "Okay. Be that way."

"I am."

• • •

Next morning came, and over a breakfast of honest-to-God eggs off the farm by way of the commissary refrigerator, Sam Sloan teased McKay. "I noticed we didn't get our throats cut in the night."

McKay sipped his coffee. It was hot and corrosive enough to eat through sheet metal; just the way he liked it. "Tomorrow's another day."

Sloan shook his head. "McKay, I just don't understand you sometimes. These people are welcoming us with open hearts. How can you not trust them?"

"Easy. They fucked over the scientists in Shawnee. They sucked up to the Effsees. What more do you need?"

"What happened in Shawnee was an oversight—had to be. Dex White isn't that kind of man, to condemn innocent men and women to their deaths. And as for backing the FSE—I seem to remember a time when you said our loyalty lay with Wild Bill Lowell."

McKay didn't say anything. Sloan was right about that last.

Tom trooped stoically off to help Casey nursemaid Mac-Gregor. Curly-headed Chris, looking anything but bureaucratic in red shorts, sandals, and tube top, turned up right after breakfast. She had a date to take Sam Sloan to go look at the Brave New World, Kansas City edition. McKay spent the day sleeping, shooting the shit with India Three, and checking certain preparations he'd made—just against a rainy day.

Sam came back bubbling over with enthusiasm for what Dexter White had wrought: "It's great. He's got all the people pulling together. They have a vitality, a sense of purpose. Shared purpose, the kind you hardly ever saw among Americans, back—" He let the words trail abruptly away.

"Sound like you're deciding it was a real grand idea to hold the One-Day War," McKay growled, looking up from a beer he'd extorted from the Mayor's commissary staff.

Sam flushed. "That's not fair!"

McKay sipped his beer and ignored him; he was a dead-end street kid from Pittsburgh, for Christ's sake; "fair" cut no ice with *him*.

After a moment Sloan looked a little shamefaced and went

on. "Maybe it came out sounding that way. But you should let Chris take you around and show you what she showed me. It might just turn your head around."

McKay raised an eyebrow. "That little friend of yours shows me what she probably showed you, Sergeant Eklund'll turn *her* head around. On her pretty little neck."

"Jesus," Sloan turned away in disgust. "Sometimes I wonder why I bother trying to discuss things with you."

"Then don't."

"Think what you will. But you'll see. We're safe here, perfectly safe."

"Right," McKay said.

And so the next morning they woke up to find themselves surrounded.

CHAPTER
TEN

Billy McKay was sitting in the second floor commissary with his booted feet propped on the cracked Formica surface of a long table, sipping boiled coffee from a foam cup when Rosie came busting in, coat-scuttle helmet askew on his bushy Afro, and the whites showing all around his eyes. "Lieutenant McKay, come quick! There're troops out in the street. They got tanks, guns—everything!"

He stopped short. It finally registered on his frightened brain that for the first time since they'd arrived, McKay was wearing urban-warfare camouflage, printed in a jagged pattern of grays and blacks and browns. McKay finished the last long, leisurely swallow and plunked the cup down on the table. "Sergeant Eklund got everybody alerted?"

Rosie's eyes were swiveling back and forth as if he expected the attackers to come flitting through the commissary's thin fiberboard walls like ghosts. "Yeah."

McKay wiped his mouth with the back of his hand and stood. He picked up his Maremont, slammed back the charging handle and let it ride forward, punching a 7.62-mm round into the chamber. "Let's do it."

It was 0430.

Already on the move, he adjusted the personal communicator buttoned in a breast pocket of his camouflaged coveralls to receive the frequency used by India Three's walkie-talkies. Tests had proven that radio communication was generally reliable in here, though there were a few dead spots scattered around the building. "Who's watching the corridors?" he asked, keying on his throat mike.

"I am." It was Chi. "Up here on the fourth floor. Buncha dudes hanging out in the central section, all got up like they going to a Halloween party."

"What the fuck does that mean?"

"Riot gear, man. Helmets with faceplates, flak jackets, M-16s, shotguns, gas."

"Police or military?"

"Shore look like police to me."

McKay had reached the stairs. He was more or less in the middle of the west wing of the complex, well away from its juncture with the base of the U. Chief Peary's men would not be nearby, unless some of them had infiltrated during the night. And since the corridors linking the two sectors had been strewn with motion detectors feeding constant streams of input to Mobile One's ever-watchful computer, and since the computer hadn't filled the Guardians' heads with the whine of an annunciator, he was pretty sure that hadn't happened. Unless all the goddamned things were on the fritz at once. That could happen. But there was not time to check it now. Fuck it and drive on.

"Okay, Chi. Keep loose and keep out of sight."

"Roger." He sounded a lot calmer than his buddy Rosie. For all his loose-goose ways, Chi was a pretty strak troop, one of the ones McKay relied on.

McKay took the steps two at a time, holding his machine gun barrel up to avoid banging it against the walls. Anyone who'd seen the mid-1980s adventure flick *Rambo* would have recognized the piece; one just like it had figured prominently in that movie in the unlikely guise of a liberated Warsaw Pact weapon. It was a Maremont Lightweight Machine Gun, stripped-down version of the old standby M-60. As early as the Vietnam War, troops in action had "field butchered" the unwieldy "pig," cutting down its cumbersome twenty-odd pound weight as much as could be done without impairing performance too much, so that they could take advantage of the weapon's potent fire power without becoming totally exhausted hauling the beast around. Subsequently the Maremont company proposed a streamlined design, and the Marine Corps adopted it as the M-60E3.

"Anybody on the fourth floor landing, don't shoot—I'm coming up." A moment later he pounded around the switchback in the stairs from the third floor and, sure enough, there was Sandy, just raising her weapon from low point. Her long black hair had been wound into a single braid and she coiled it once around her head. Her face was very white. "I thought we were safe," she said. "I never thought they'd do this."

"We ain't safe," McKay said. "Not anywhere. Not ever." He drove on up the stairs.

On the top floor Sam Sloan was watching the corridor that connected with the complex's central section while Casey and Tom guarded the President. The apartments occupied the middle of the wing on both sides of the corridor. The facilities in the other wing were the mirror image of these; it had been White's last-minute decision to have his office moved to the southeast corner of the whole complex, where he could look out at his domain instead of staring straight into the face of the rest of the Center. According to the ever-helpful Chris, he did however occupy a set of apartments identical to the ones in this wing.

Despite Tom and Casey's repeated urgings, MacGregor was up, wearing jeans and a red-checked Pendleton shirt he'd hastily pulled on, peering down at the street and the red-paved plaza through the big polarized glass window.

He turned as McKay came thumping in. "You were right all along, McKay." He sounded subdued. "I never thought they'd do it."

"Could you stand a little back from the window, Mr. President? There ain't no light in here, but it's still dark enough outside somebody could be watching with a night-vision enhancer. We don't want 'em spotting you."

MacGregor blinked and stepped back. Ignoring his own warning, McKay walked right up to the glass.

There they were. Just as he'd always known they would be.

Men in berets and bulky flak jackets bailing out of canvas-backed trucks, a Bradley Infantry Fighting Vehicle—known as an IFT—parked spang at the center of the U's mouth, its 25-millimeter gun aimed right up at the center of the west wing.

Right about the center of my belt buckle, McKay thought in amusement, pulling out a cigar. There was even a 105-millimeter howitzer out there, being hurriedly uncoupled from the jeep that had towed it into position. Dawn light was beginning to spill along the street from the east like thin sour milk.

"It's like this on the other two sides of the building, too, Billy," Rogers said quietly. "Looks like a hundred twenty, thirty men."

"They got us pretty well socked in," Casey added.

McKay grinned a slow grin. The Effsees had them penned in, sure enough. But they were chickenshits. They hadn't done it the bold, balls-to-the-wall way, with a silent infiltration and a quick raging rush. It was a risky way, grant it—even if the Guardians' suspicions were lulled, there was no way they were going to totally slack their alertness, and they could be expected to inflict maximum hurt upon any kind of attacking force, no matter how quiet their approach. But it would have done the trick. Instead, their commander—probably at Mayor White's insistence, certainly to his relief—had decided to do it this way. A straight showdown: cow the little knot of men and women holed up inside the echoing emptiness of the complex with a totally overwhelming show of force.

Right.

"Billy." It was Sloan. "You were right. You were right all along. It's a trap. And we walked right into it. With our eyes wide open."

Never had McKay heard Sloan's voice filled with such bitterness, self-disgust, and defeat. He felt sorry for his teammate, almost sorry enough to cut him some slack. But not quite. "I oughta hate to say this," he said, "but I don't. I fucking told you so."

The phone rang. With an odd little frown, MacGregor moved to the desk, picked it up. "Yes?"

"This is Dexter White," that familiar smooth baritone rolled out the desk speaker. "The only choice you have is to surrender, Jeff. I'm sorry."

Sudden weariness flooded Jeff MacGregor's veins as if he'd suddenly been shot full of mercury. "I don't think I can do that, Dex," he said, so softly the other men in the room could barely hear him.

"It's really the best thing, Jeff. You don't have a chance in there. We really don't want anyone to be hurt."

MacGregor dropped chin to collarbone, shut his eyes, dropped the knuckles of his left hand onto the desktop to help bear his weight. "Why?"

A pause. "Unity."

A frown sank into MacGregor's features as if etching itself on the front of his skull. "What? I don't understand."

"Unity, Jeff. One world. What we've worked for all these years—in the Movement, boring from within the system. The FSE was well on its way to putting this country back together, even if it was under that old reactionary Lowell—and their leadership had assured me that his days as a voice in American politics were numbered. They're offering us confederation, solidarity with what they're doing in Europe. And after that—" Unbelievably a chuckle, full-throated and rich, flowed out of the speaker. "After that, who knows? Maybe we can give this whole old world the single strong government she's needed for so long."

Casey mouthed the words, *their leadership?* MacGregor nodded. "Their leadership, you said. Would that be—?"

"Maximov. Yevgeny Maximov. A great man, a visionary genius. I've been an associate member of his Internationalist Council for many years. He's what we need, Jeff. What humanity needs."

"Holy shit," McKay said. He didn't even bother to try to whisper.

"You'll be well treated, Jeff. I have their assurance. There'll be a jet to fly you to exile in Europe. Quite a cushy exile, I must say; a villa on the Riviera, servants, all your needs attended to. Certainly better than the pillar-to-post existence that faces you here."

"What about my people?"

"Sergeant Eklund's platoon will be disarmed and transported anywhere they desire within a one-hundred-kilometer radius—and their weapons returned to them on release."

"And the Guardians?"

Another pause. "Why, they, they'll have to be debriefed, of course—"

"I think not, Dex. But thank you anyway." Before the startled Mayor could reply MacGregor hung up the telephone.

Outside the troops were deploying in the street, falling flat along the curb, fading back into the parking garage. McKay frowned at that. He had been expecting it, but he hoped they wouldn't go too high.

Sitting in the commander's cupola of the Bradley was a man wearing an orange beret. He must have been in touch with White, because the phone connection had scarcely been broken when he held up a microphone to his lips and spoke. The loudspeaker affixed to the IFV boomed out: "This is Colonel Derkszoon, commanding Company A of the First Battalion of the Second Federated States of Europe Expeditionary Force Airmobile Brigade. I am calling upon Vice President Jeffrey MacGregor and his followers to lay down their arms and come out peacefully." He spoke excellent English, clear, but with a marked accent. "You have sixty seconds."

McKay looked at Tom, rolled his eyes upward. "Keep him talking, Mr. President," he said. "Tom, this is where we came in."

Before a startled MacGregor could react the two Guardians had pushed out the door. McKay scooped up the MP-5 with integral silencer that Tom Rogers had thoughtfully left lying on the receptionist's desk. He slung the M-60. Rogers already had his MP-5 in hand and a CAWS slung over his back.

As they made their way quickly down a hall lit with pale sun falling through a skylight, Sloan asked, "Where are you going, McKay?"

"Pay a little social call."

A little exploration the day before had confirmed something McKay already suspected. If there was one area people designing security factors into the building plan would fall down on, it was going to be the roof. That was the case here at the Martin Luther King Memorial Center. Access to the roof locked from the inside, of course. And that was about that. They were just normal metal doors, the skylights just glass.

One place White's boys were almost certain to be watching though were the two doors that gave onto the west wing roof. So McKay and Rogers took an elevator.

They pried open the door to the shaft. The car itself was somewhere below them. All they had to do then was to scale the metal rungs of the ladder leading up to the top of the shaft—where McKay, yesterday, had carefully hacksawed the padlock securing the door to outside. The day before they had been attacked. Rogers went first, slipping out into cloud-filtered daylight to peer around the corner of the housing. "Three guards, Billy. At the little divider wall between this wing and the central one."

"How far apart are they?"

"Spaced about five meters." McKay heard a touch of amusement in the dry voice. The riot police probably thought they were spread out all to hell and gone, when one good grenade burst would get them all. Not that McKay and Rogers were going to use anything as noisy as grenades, just yet.

Not that even grenades might give them away—not with the commotion that goddamn giant windmill was putting out. The creaking and banging of the contraption beat on McKay like fists. He could see why the Downtown Neighborhood Association got pissed.

He boosted his bulk up and out. He glanced around. Good. They weren't near enough to the edge of the roof that any of the Effsees in the street could spot them. He and Rogers began to move along the roof toward the juncture of the sections, moving in short dashes from cover to cover. The roof itself was not only broken up with elevator housings and the humped forms of ventilation units, a fair forest of stubby pipes and ducts; it also had the mast of the windmill and all these damn solar arrays sprouting all over it. There was no way you could get any kind of decent sight lines over any distance at all.

Just what the doctor ordered for would-be infiltrators.

From down below in the street the two men heard the echoing sounds of electronically augmented voices arguing back and forth, even above the din of the vast blades rotating in the desultory morning breeze. Jeff MacGregor, his voice relayed to Mobile One and piped out, amplified, through the vehicle's own speakers, was negotiating with the FSE colonel. What he was saying McKay couldn't tell and didn't care.

He and Rogers worked their way to within twenty meters of the low rampart that divided the two sections of the building. McKay hunkered down behind an air-conditioning unit, Rogers behind a square silver metal duct. They looked at each other, nodded. There was no need for words.

As one, each man thrust the stubby muzzle of his sub-machine gun around the corner of his cover and fired a single quiet shot. The police officers at either end died with holes drilled through their heads even as their startled eyes registered the sight of two men poking guns at them a stone's throw away. The third man gaped. "What the hell?" he yelled, and brought his rifle to his shoulder.

Two short bursts knocked him sprawling onto his back.

While Rogers covered, McKay raced forward, vaulted the low wall. He crouched down behind a cement piling at the base of an array of solar collectors and looked at the sprawling bodies of the police officers. "Fucking shame," he commented. They'd just been doing their duty, after all.

Without a word, Rogers passed him, moving for cover at the windmill's base.

On the fifth floor of the west wing, in what had for slightly less than forty-eight hours been the office of the President of the United States, Casey Wilson sat at the edge of the desk holding his Remington 700 sniper's rifle negligently in his lap while MacGregor dickered with the Dutch colonel. Casey sat well back from the window, but he could see the edge of the plaza and the men lying in the street with their guns trained on them. He was totally relaxed; he'd already imposed that strange calm with which he went to battle on himself, without consciously thinking about it.

MacGregor stared at the microphone in his hand as if he wasn't sure where he'd got it. "This isn't going to work," he said, and indeed the colonel's voice rattling the big glass was beginning to sound impatient. "They're going to start shooting at any minute. I sure hope McKay knows what he is doing."

Casey smiled at him. "He generally does, Mr. President."

●   ●   ●

"I sure hope McKay knows what the hell he's doing," Corporal James Tall Bear grunted.

Marla Eklund surveyed her people. With the exception of Chi, still skulking in an office keeping an eye on the police in the central section, they were all lying on their bellies in the corridor that ran the length of the wing. "If they're shooting, we won't be able to shoot back none," the giant black named Jamake said. "Craziest thing I ever heard."

"It's what McKay told us to do," Eklund said. She was standing up with her helmet on and her M-16 in her hand.

"Does McKay run this squad?" Tall Bear asked.

Eklund fixed him with a cool blue eye. "While we're together, he sure does," she said. "That bother you, Corporal?"

Tall Bear shrugged.

Casey slipped off the side of the desk and stood. "We better be on our way, Mr. President."

"What? What do you mean?" Colonel Derkszoon's voice was droning through a countdown outside. MacGregor's most earnest negotiation had only bought them another minute, and that was fast running out.

"We're going down. To ground level."

"Why?"

Casey laid his hand on the President's shoulder and gently urged him out of the room. "You're going to hang out in the foyer, out of sight," he said, "and I'm going to make a break for the car, when McKay gives me the word."

MacGregor stared at him. "That's suicide."

"We'll see, man."

McKay and Rogers had almost reached the east wing when the count hit thirty. "Shit," McKay said with feeling. He and Rogers were both crouched behind an elevator housing. A couple of guards stood in plain sight on the roof in front of them, weapons slung, looking down into the street below. "Okay. Sam, are you there?"

"Here, McKay."

"When I give the word, pull back out of there to the next stairwell down from the central section. Then head downstairs."

"Downstairs?"

"That's affirmative. Casey will be in Mobile One's turret when you get there. You're going to drive for him."

He could almost feel Sloan's confusion. He was giving what sounded like a set of totally suicidal orders. But for once Sloan, usually the most inclined to talk back, had no questions except, "How do I know when you give the word?"

"You'll know. Case?"

"Here, Billy. I'm in position."

"That's what I needed to know. You wait for my word too. Eklund?" he said, changing the setting on his communicator.

"Eklund here."

"Tell Chi to start pulling back. When the party starts, hold your people in the corridor ten-fifteen seconds to let the Effsees get their first volley out of the way. Then move forward and open fire. Tell them not to bother aiming—just spray bullets all over everywhere. And keep their heads the hell down."

"That's affirmative, McKay. But I must say you are the craziest damn Yankee I have ever met."

"Roger that."

"*Sixty!*" Colonel Derkszoon's voice thundered in the street. "*Open fire!*" The 25-millimeter cannon in the Bradley's cupola cut loose in a snarling burst. The polarized windows of the President's erstwhile offices exploded in powdered-glass snow and great green shards. The howitzer boomed, punching a hole through a precast concrete panel and totally obliterating the third-floor ladies' john. From three sides of the building, the hundred and twenty-four men of the expeditionary force company opened fire on King Center's beleaguered west wing.

Bill McKay took a small transmitter from the other breast pocket of his coveralls, blew away a residue of tobacco flecks from the cigars he kept in the pocket, flipped up the safety cover, pressed a button.

Lying in a corridor junction staring toward the detachment of city police officers in riot gear hunkered not a hundred feet away, Sloan was suddenly deafened by a crackle of what sounded like gunfire. Instantly his view of the cops was wiped away by a wall of white smoke. His eyes and the membranes inside his nose began to tingle. *Tear gas!* he knew. "Billy, what the hell—?"

Vibrating through the floor came other reports. Then came a thin screaking sound followed by a thud that jarred his bones, and the firefight noise suddenly stopped.

He was staring at a clear glass wall with the smoke—and the Kansas City police officers—on the other side of it. As he watched, the glass vibrated slightly to a burst of automatic-rifle fire. It didn't even chip.

"CS cans and some firefight simulators left over from Heartland," McKay's voice said in his ear. "Wired them up and placed them yesterday while you were off watching Miss Chris shake her pretty ass. The barrier down?"

Sloan could barely find his voice. "Affirmative," he croaked.

"Great, go for it. Give 'er five, then you go too, Case." Without waiting for a response, he punched a button on his communicator and straightened, then took one step away from the elevator housing, slinging the MP-5 and releasing the M-60.

"Okay, outlaws," McKay bellowed, "*rock and roll!*"

Crouched down behind the counter of the information booth on the ground floor, Casey Wilson saw a sudden bright flash illuminate the top floor of the derelict parking garage across the street. A white arrow of smoke streaked down to hit Colonel Derkszoon's IFV just behind the turret. The shaped charge of the RPG-7V rocket penetrated the armor, detonated the munitions stowage, and blew the colonel out of the cupola like a cork out of a bottle. At the same instant, muzzle flashes began to dance like fireflies all along the fifth-floor deck.

In the street, the Dutch FSE troopers began to holler as the bullets from behind found their flesh. A pair of troopers wrestled with their colonel, trying to smother the flames that wrapped him, hastily tearing off their fatigue blouses to muffle the fire. The Bradley was exploding with a series of great flaming volcanic belches; nobody got out.

Casey hit the door at the run. Hardly anyone was looking his way. Nothing in this wide green world freaks out a unit on the firing line so much as being shot up from behind. He raced to the armored car, spun in mid-stride, slammed with his back against its steel and titanium flank, wrenched open the door, and threw himself inside. Laying down his rifle on the perforated steel deck, he swarmed up into the turret and began to crank it around manually. A thin clanging sound told him small-arms fire was bouncing off the hull. But nothing big—yet.

Casey's every instinct rebelled against being stuck here, in this squat monster, immobile, helpless, earthbound. He was still more used to being strapped into the cocoonlike cockpit of an F-16D, a fantastically agile fighter aircraft, ready to leap with enormous power in response to the slightest stimulus. To expose himself here to a firing line that had to be crawling with antitank weapons—that was just asking for death. But he did it, and he did it without thinking about it. He was a Guardian.

McKay and Sloan both ran flat out, vaulting the wall between the U's base and the east wing that was Mayor White's stronghold. A sentry's peripheral vision caught motion. He swung, shouted, slapped his buddy on the arm and then fumbled for his M-16. McKay stopped and shot them down with a burst from the hip. Then he was running again, dodging the struts of the solar panels. Tom Rogers was ahead of him, fumbling at his belt as he neared Mayor Dexter White's corner office.

At the sound of automatic cannon fire ticking discreetly but distinctly through the soundproofing of his office, Mayor White raised his head from where he had been staring without focus at his desktop. "It's begun."

Ambrose's mouth compressed more tightly shut. "Why couldn't those reactionary idiots have surrendered?" he asked bitterly. "Think of the damage that's being done to our facility."

White turned his head and looked at him. "Think of the damage it's doing to the people in there," remarked Chief Peary in a soft voice. He was standing over by the wall, framed in weak light from the skylight.

Ambrose glowered at him. "I don't mean to criticize, Chief, but why aren't you off with your men supervising the cordoning-off of this area? Our plans for alliance with the FSE will be severely set back if through clumsiness we permit anyone to escape."

Peary gave him a cool-eyed look. "Nobody's getting out of that," he said quietly.

"He's here because I asked him here, Charles. If you're uncomfortable here, perhaps you can go down to the shelters," White said.

The skylight exploded down with a crash. The eyes of all three men fixed in fascinated horror on the small cylinder bouncing in the center of the rug.

The room vanished in white light and thunder.

CHAPTER
ELEVEN ─────────────

"Yeeee—*hah!*" With a ringing rebel yell Eklund led her people at the charge into the offices overlooking the embattled plaza. The glass in the outside windows was supposedly bulletproof. But the raking fire by the expeditionary force soldiers' heavy automatic weapons had blasted most of them to shreds. The squaddies poked their M-16s out past jagged fangs of glass and cut loose at the soldiers milling frantically in the street. Despite McKay's instructions simply to bust caps as fast as possible, Tall Bear took careful aim with an M-203 and dropped a high explosive 40-millimeter round smack in the middle of the howitzer's crew, which was dithering in the middle of the street trying to decide whether to keep firing at their objective or to traverse the gun around to shoot at their unexpected attackers in their rear.

It was a nice shot but academic. The grenade had scarcely gone off, leaving two gunners in bloody rags and a third sitting on the ground staring in mute astonishment at the spurting stumps where his hands had been, when Casey opened up with the two turret guns in the V-450. At this range, less than a hundred meters, the 708-grain slugs from the .50-caliber would almost turn a man inside out. And the 40-millimeter grenades of the M-19 were lethal out to the one-kilometer limit of their range. The lucky soldiers who had managed to take cover on the first two stories of the parking garage found their luck had run out as white phosphorus grenades began to seek for them with searing starfish fingers, HEDP grenades to blast them with chunks of shattered masonry, .50-caliber rounds to punch through the walls with sufficient force to knock a fist-sized hole through both sides of a man.

It wasn't all one way. It never is. A few Effsee troopers, braver than the rest, kept up a sporadic fire at their objective. A 5.56-round, slim and sharp as a needle, poked through Private Gillespie's right eye, drilled his brain, and knocked out a thumb-sized shard of skull before penetrating the swept rear skirt of this helmet. The wiry, curly-headed rifleman never even had time to be surprised.

Out in the middle of the street, one of the two men who'd put out Colonel Derkszoon was helping the badly burned officer limp to safety through a hail of fire. His buddy lay with his own scorched blouse draped over his chest, decapitated by a single round from Casey's M-2. The Effsees out in front of Martin Luther King, Jr., Memorial Center had had enough. Those that could, simply turned and ran; those that couldn't crawl, lay where they were and groaned.

Standing in a strange sensory-deprivation haze of deafness-blindness-numbness, Dexter White became aware of a rough hand gripping his right arm by the biceps. Reflexively he resisted. In response he felt something hard thrust into the soft flesh below his shortribs. It might have been a broomstick. Under the circumstances he was willing to bet it was the muzzle of a gun.

Ambrose had fallen down to the carpet and was lying on his side kicking with a strange pedaling motion, holding both hands to his cheeks and squalling. Recognizing the flash-boom stun grenade for what it was, Chief Peary had almost managed to shut his eyes in time. Not quite; now he was fumbling for his .357 Magnum in its shoulder holster, blinking at great purple and green balls of light that flitted across his eyes when somebody grabbed him by the shirt and threw him up against the wall. A gun muzzle buried itself in his belly, pinning him there like a bug on a board, while his assailant plucked his Smith and Wesson out of the holster for him.

His vision clearing, he made out the huge but unmistakable outline of Billy McKay. "Listen up, Chief. I could shoot that 'thing"—a headshake towards Ambrose—"and not lose no sleep over it. But I'd sure hate to waste a good man like you. So don't try nothing, okay?"

Rogers had the Mayor's hands tied behind his back with his own necktie. "Billy, if he can, he's going to follow us."

"Oh." Struck by some inspiration, McKay quickly frisked the man, came up with his cuffs, and chained him to the Mayor's desk.

White had recovered his wits, if not all his sight and hearing. "Go ahead and shoot me now," he said, his voice shaken but firm. "Whatever it is you have in mind, I won't go along with it."

"Sure you will, Mr. Mayor." There was something about the voice of the man who held him—whom he now realized was Rogers, the former Green Beret—that chilled him to the core. It was quiet, polite, deferential—and turned his blood to ice.

"Don't you have the idea yet, Dex?" McKay asked. "We got us a hostage."

The troops on the streets that ran behind and along the side of the west wing held their positions. They had heard their comrades' barrage cut loose a minute before, and heard the sudden, totally unexpected volume of answering fire. The colonel had reserved to his own contingent the honor of storming the Center and making the American vice president captive. His men had been ordered in no uncertain terms to stay where they were and not rush the building unless directly ordered to. Since the price of disobedience in the FSE's armies tended to be swift in application, lingering in accomplishment, and ultimately lethal, they did what they were damned well told, even though the ones on the side streets could see their buddies being massacred.

But there's always *somebody* . . .

•   •   •

Having automatically pulled on the gunner's earphones to deaden the eardrum-busting racket with the guns, Casey felt rather than heard Sam Sloan climb into the vehicle, felt the engine cough into life as Sloan hit the starter. "We're in, Case. Jeff's with me."

"Casey, Sam," McKay's voice vibrated through his mastoid process. "We're coming down. Come make pickup."

"Roger, McKay." The vehicle began to move.

"Casey! Azimuth 345—shoot!" Marching with one hand wrapped in Dexter White's collar, gun swiveling this way and that like an insect's feelers, and with Rogers walking ahead of him in his slow methodical way making sure the way was clear, McKay was taking the little party toward the stairs nearest the west face of the east wing. It was fortunate that he did, because through the cool polarized glass he could see the boxy little Highly Maneuverable Military Vehicle bombing around the corner of the west wing, ready to blast Mobile One with its own pintle-mounted M-19.

The speedy little HMMV came on spitting High-Explosive, Dual-Purpose grenades that combined shaped-charged punch with high-explosive killing power. The automatic launcher drew an irregular line of explosions across the glass of the first floor of the central section and the figured cement of the second. Knowing only generally where his target was, the FSE gunner was probing for it with a steady hosing stream of fire.

To play it safe, Casey should have held back both triggers and spun the turret to the angle McKay had given him. But marksmanship had been one of Casey's many prides as a fighter jock. With a cool resolve that would have turned Sam Sloan's hair white if he'd had any inkling of it, Casey snapped the turret around to aim north northwest, caught the HMMV in his sights as it came screaming into view on two tires, led it slightly, and triggered a precise three-round burst.

The combat car became a hurtling orange fireball. The gunner standing in the ringmount threw up his hands as the vehicle heeled over farther and farther to the left—either to ward off the flames that leapt avidly for throat and face or to shield himself from the imminent impact with the pavement. Then the vehicle lost it altogether, came off its wheels and rolled, pinching the gunner in two at the waist, wiping out half a dozen soldiers before slamming into the entrance of the parking garage.

"Let's go, Sam," Casey said.

The big 450 came bucking to a halt in front of the east wing's entryway. Leaving White in Rogers's custody in the foyer, McKay stepped out into the building heat of the day. He started to duck back at a sudden pop-pop-pop from the street, then realized it was ammunition cooking off one of the vehicles burning out there. No one was shooting from the street anymore. It didn't look as if anyone was still alive.

He turned back and held the door open. "After you, Mr. Mayor," he said as Tom marched the captive White out. Mobile One's side door swung open.

"You'll never get away with this—this act of brigandage," White said. "Does your President MacGregor know what kind of crimes you are committing in his name?"

"Come on aboard, Dex, and we'll talk about it," came a familiar voice from inside the vehicle. White stopped, frowned. He leaned forward, frowning as he squinted into the gloom inside the armored car.

Sitting on a fold-down seat aft of the turret root, Jeffrey MacGregor grinned at his longtime friend and political ally. "Have a seat." Before the startled Mayor could react Rogers and McKay had hustled him into the car and slammed the door.

McKay moved to the other side of the vehicle and slid up the steel shutter of an armored glass view slit. India Three's truck remained parked a hundred meters away across the plaza. "Eklund? What the hell's going on? We got to move."

"We've got trouble, McKay. Truck's all shot to heck. She ain't moving anywhere, not under her own power."

Sloan looked back over his shoulder, alarmed. But McKay just nodded, reached up to diddle the dial on his personal communicator, mumbled words that no one else heard because he'd cut himself out of the Guardians' comm circuit. Then he dialed them and Marla back into the conversation. "I think we can help you out, Eklund. Sloan, drive us over between the truck and the street. Case, you cover, and if you see a vehicle coming out of the garage, don't shoot unless you're damn sure it's hostile."

"Roger, Billy."

He settled his bulk into the ESO's seat. His teammates and MacGregor kept throwing him these very curious glances. White, who didn't know enough about what was going on to wonder about it, continued to fume. "This is insupportable! And you know you'll never get out of Kansas City. Chief Peary's men have this entire area sealed off. And they have the means to deal with this precious armored car of yours, never fear!"

Tom Rogers showed him a thin-lipped expression that could almost have been called a smile. "We reckoned that, Mr. Mayor. Why else do you think we brought you along?" White opened his mouth, shut it, slumped back against the hull of the vehicle, wincing at the noise as Mobile One's ten tons and cleated tires chewed up the pavement. The gray in his sideburns seemed to have started seeping into the rest of his face.

"What I want to know," Sam Sloan said, "is just where the heck we're going to get a new vehicle for Marla's people."

"From the parking garage," McKay said. "Where else?"

Sloan was so startled that he actually turned his head to look back at McKay. "But all that's in there are wrecks."

"Negative. Hizzoner has some vehicles stashed there. Isn't that right, Mr. Mayor?" White looked off toward the rear of the vehicle.

"But who the hell is going to be bringing it out?"

"Probably the same people who opened up on the colonel and his men from the rear, Sam," Casey said from the turret.

"Oh."

Sloan parked the car facing the street, its tailgate a few meters from the defunct truck's. Marla and several of the others crouched by the truck, scanning the street warily, their rifles ready. They heard the sound of an engine echoing inside the cavernous emptiness of the parking garage, heard the slight squeal of tires as it came down the ramp from the top floor. It appeared, a Mercedes panel truck with yellow cab and silver box, swerving around the still-burning wreck of the HMMV and bombing across the street. They heard another distinctive sound: the growl of numerous motorcycle engines.

The truck came banging up the curb and rolled across the abused flagstones to screech to a halt right next to Eklund's vehicle. Blinking, Eklund straightened, and found herself staring through the window into the blue-green lynx eyes of the platinum-haired Desperado girl, Caprice. The girl grinned and waved. "Hop in."

And here they came, a score of chopped lean cycles, boiling out the entryway of the parking garage. In the lead rode Dreadlock Callahan, steering with one hand, holding an RPG launcher with the other. "Quite the surprise party you put on, McKay," he commented as he pulled up by the Super Commando.

"The Effsees weren't the only ones who were surprised," Sam Sloan said, letting the words go out over the car's external speaker. Callahan grinned.

"The Effsees have pulled back, at least on that side street. But sooner or later they're going to regroup and try again—especially when they get to thinking what's going to happen to them if they let us slip through their fingers."

Surprised or not, India Three boarded the new truck quickly enough. The convoy set out north, away from the remnants of the FSE encirclement force, which had pulled back to west and south. Mobile One took the lead, not only because if they ran into trouble its armorplate and tremendous firepower would give it a lot better survivability than the bikes had, but because sooner or later they were going to run into—

"Police roadblock, McKay," Sloan said after four blocks, slowing the bulk of Mobile One with deft touches of the brakes. White sat a little straighter in his seat.

"Armored vehicle, halt immediately."

Ahead McKay could see two blue-and-white cruisers parked nose to nose across the street. It wasn't the cleverest way to build a roadblock—a driver with the balls and eye and a heavy enough car could hit the junction dead center, push both out of the way, and with a little luck keep right on cruising. McKay suspected they were just there for symbolic value; no matter how they were set up, mere police cruisers were not going to slow down ten thousand kilos of armored car for very long.

"Halt where you are and surrender. We have antitank weapons trained on your vehicle. Come out peaceably and you won't—"

"We have the Mayor," Casey Wilson's voice said cheerily through the loudspeaker.

"—be harmed. What did you say?"

"We have the Mayor."

McKay flicked on a forward audio pickup, a computer-filtered shotgun mike. There was some heavy-duty dissension going on behind that barricade. "Maybe you'd better talk to them, Mr. Mayor," he said, swiveling his seat and holding out a mike.

White gave him a hot black glare. McKay didn't flinch, the microphone didn't waver. The Mayor got out of his chair, walked forward slightly bent over to take the microphone in his hand. "This is Mayor Dexter White," he said. His voice seemed to catch periodically, as if he had something sharp in his throat snagging the words on their way out. "I—please let these vehicles pass unmolested."

Dexter White was a proud man, and the words clearly cost him a great deal. For some reason McKay started feeling sorry for him. "Thank you, Mr. Mayor," was all he could think of to say.

From the look that earned him, he was just thinking his concern wasn't appreciated when a second amplified voice boomed, "How do we know that's Mayor White talking?"

"What, do they think I'm fucking Rich Little?" McKay snarled. "Tom, pop the side hatch and let them get a good look at His Nibs."

A flicker of expression crossed White's face like a wisp of cloud across the sun. "Don't even think about it, Mr. Mayor. Tommy's got the reflexes of a mongoose. You wouldn't make it five meters."

White smiled at him. "And where would you be without your hostage, Mr. McKay?"

"Your Honor, we been through every antiterrorist training course known to man, plus a few they only teach in the Twilight Zone. Don't try to tell *us* about hostage situations.

"First, you make a break, you're out of life. Second, just think what this big old armored car could do to your precious cops—and even if they nail us, how about India Three and those outlaw bikers you saw? These people are armed to the eyeballs, brother. They could burn out half of downtown KC before you chopped them all."

The door was opened and Mayor White allowed to step down onto the asphalt beside the vehicle, with Sam Sloan holding on to his arm with one hand and holding the muzzle of his Galil Short Assault Rifle pressed against the Mayor's neck with the other. That closed the debate with Kansas City's finest. They pulled back the cars and solemnly waved the convoy through.

Within two blocks the streets started to fill up with pedestrians, bicyclists, and handcarts, going about their daily business. It was a pattern McKay and Rogers well knew from their field days. People adjust. After the first shock of exposure to violence, you find them totally ignoring full-scale battles going on scant blocks away, whether they're in Beirut, Managua, or Kansas City.

"I still want to know how you pulled this particular rabbit out of your hat, McKay," Sloan said, veering to avoid a fat man pushing a bicycle with a plastic washtub heaped with canned goods balanced on seat and handlebars, Vietnamese-style. "What the hell were Callahan and his people doing in that parking garage, for God's sake? And what—"

"Sam," Casey said, "haven't you figured it out yet? We've been, like, set up, man."

"Set up?" Both MacGregor and White echoed.

"Yeah, man—uh, Mr. President. That whole thing, the falling-out with Callahan's people over them not being able to come into KC with us—it was all put on. The Desperadoes hung back awhile, then infiltrated into KC after dark, then into that garage."

McKay was laughing out loud; he couldn't help himself. "Good, Casey, real good. You make me proud."

"Why didn't we hear their engines?" MacGregor wanted to know.

"Inside a building that heavily soundproofed, Mr. President?" Sloan asked. "But there were people out and around until fairly late at night, and almost certainly a city police foot patrol around the outside of the complex. Why didn't *they* hear anything?''

"With that fucking windmill banging around right over their heads?" McKay asked. "Get serious. Callahan's people kept their speed nice and low and their engines quiet, and Mayor White's pride and joy did the rest!''

MacGregor was shaking his head. "And let me guess the rest. You gave Mr. Callahan a special frequency on which he could talk to you and you alone.''

"Right the first time, Mr. President.''

"But why?''

McKay chewed on his lip a bit. That was a hard one to answer. It involved cascading loyalties: he didn't dare tell his teammates about the plan because one of them might have felt morally bound to tell the President—the man they were bound to serve and protect, their Commander in Chief, in fact the only authority to which they were answerable according to the Secret Act of Congress that created Project Guardian. And if President MacGregor knew, he would probably in turn have felt bound to tell his friend and host Dexter White about the intrusion . . . and that would have been all she wrote.

"Well, Mr. President—" McKay began, not really sure exactly what in hell he was going to say.

"Talking of engine noises," Sam Sloan said suddenly, hunkering over the wheel and trying to peer upward through the narrow vision block, "does anyone else hear a helicopter?''

And the Walgreen's on the ground floor across the intersection ahead of them blew up.

CHAPTER
TWELVE ———————————

A file of explosions danced along the street before them, throwing black chunks of asphalt and bikes and bodies up into the air. The throngs that had been staring in open curiosity at the odd procession now fled screaming, the smart ones ducking into buildings, the foolish and the panicked stampeding along the street. Sloan pushed the accelerator to the floor and cranked the wheel hard left, desperate to get out of the line of fire of whatever in hell's name was shooting at them. Mobile One screamed as it took the corner, leaning way over despite its mammoth suspension.

A young woman in a bandana and a patched smock stood frozen in the act of crossing the street, clutching the hand of a five-year-old girl. For all the speed of his reflexes Sam Sloan only had time to register the look of doomed horrified disbelief on the mother's face, and then the giant car ran them down. Everybody inside heard her short shriek punctuated by a double thump of bodies against the hull.

"Murderers!" Mayor White exclaimed, froth flying from his lips. He lunged forward, hands clawing for Sloan. McKay turned in his seat and backhanded him across the face, knocking him to the deck. He rolled hard against the side of the compartment as Sloan screeched around another corner, lay there moaning softly.

"Hypocritical sonofabitch," McKay said. The enemy gunfire had torn at least half a dozen innocent passersby to shreds. Sam's face ran with helpless tears.

"Anybody know what the hell's after us?" McKay called on all channels.

It all happened too quickly even for Casey to track the turret around in time. But he had caught a glimpse of their assailant through the 360-degree periscope in the turret. "Chopper, Billy," he replied. "Bell OH-58."

"Eklund? Callahan? Anybody hurt?"

Two negatives rapped back. "They were shooting at you, McKay," Eklund said. "Seem to have some sort of automatic cannon."

"Weapons pod," Rogers said. "Automatic grenade launcher, I'll bet."

"Great," McKay said. Forty-millimeter HEDP rounds fired from above would peel open Mobile One's thinner top armor like a giant can opener. "Callahan, clear your people the hell out of here as fast as they can ride. Eklund, we are heading west. You head somewhere else. We'll draw their fire; we have a chance, you don't."

"Negative, McKay. We'll draw their fire. You've got the President."

"*Fuck* that, Eklund. They know we have MacGregor. They won't dick with you unless—" A bright flash washed across his view slit and a shower of masonry and broken glass cascaded across Mobile One's sloping front deck. The chopper hovered at an intersection two blocks ahead like a giant predatory insect. But this time by sheer good chance Casey's turret happened to be pointing in roughly the right direction. The big car rocked to the tremendous recoil of the two automatic weapons, and the helicopter vanished as if by magic.

"Did you hit it?" Sam asked eagerly.

"I don't think so, Sam."

"He saw the muzzle flashes and booked," McKay said. "All right, Eklund, he's on our asses now. You get clear."

"Ah hear you."

"Don't give me that shit, Eklund. You've got your orders. Now *clear out!*"

"All right, damn it, we'll comply. Eklund out."

So now it was down to them. The armored car, massively protected and armed, but compared to its foe a clumsy lumbering beast. The helicopter, fast, flitting, elusive, but so fragile that a good burst of .50 caliber fire or a single round from the M-19 would bring it flaming to the ground. If it had been a dedicated combat chopper, an AH-64 or an old Cobra, it wouldn't have been much contest at all; those ships were designed to bag much bigger game than Mobile One.

But the FSE expeditionary force was starting to really scrape for resources. Attrition among front-line battle choppers had been heavy in the conventional fighting between NATO and Warsaw Pact forces that preceded the One-Day War. The best the small garrison left behind in Kansas City could muster was an old Kiowa Light Observation Helicopter with a grenade-launcher pod bolted to its left side. Not the sort of thing you wanted to throw in the path of the Eighth Guards Army—but almost certainly more than sufficient to knock out an armored car trapped in the steel and concrete canyons of a city center.

"Tom, take the ESO seat," McKay said, pushing out of the swivel chair. "I'm going to give Casey a hand." He grabbed up his machine gun, popped the overhead hatch behind the turret, thrust his head and shoulders out into the humid breeze, holding the Maremont by front and rear pistol grips like an oversized Eliot Ness tommy gun.

Not a moment too soon. The Kiowa came buzzing out in a sideslip scarcely forty meters behind, into the intersection they'd just crossed, whining like an angry hornet. McKay pressed the black steel buttplate into his shoulder and held back the trigger. The chopper pilot let his slip carry him across the intersection and out of sight without even firing a shot.

McKay grinned. The chopper jock's eye and brain had registered muzzle flashes going off practically in his face; keyed to piano-wire tautness, his hand reacted automatically, before he realized that it wasn't the awesome turret armament that was shooting at him but a measly M-60. McKay's LWMG could bring down the Kiowa too, but the helicopter was designed to withstand a fair amount of the best punishment the 7.62-mm weapon could mete out.

"Fuck this," McKay said. "We're playing hide-and-seek with our foot in a bucket. Stop it here, Sloan." The edge of the hatch bit into his back as Sloan slewed the armored car to a halt in the middle of the block. "That will throw him off for a moment—he thinks we're hauling ass." He boosted himself up onto the rear deck, peered over the front of the turret. He had a vague idea of what he was looking for. He hoped he'd find it.

"Billy, what are they doing?" Casey asked. "Don't they know we have the Mayor with us?"

"These are the Effsees, son. They don't give shit if they blow Dexter White's fat ass away along with ours. Why do you think I didn't try the hostage rap on that colonel back there?" He hoped the Mayor was really appreciating his allies' payback of his cooperation. "Sloan, pull up another block. I think I see what I'm looking for."

Hunting, the chopper cruised out into an intersection just in time for the copilot to spot their quarry ducking back into a street two blocks to their left. *Gotcha*, he thought.

Quietly, applying only the minimum forward cyclic, the airborne hunter circled around. The pilot made for a spot two blocks behind the place they had spotted the big armored car. If their quarry was backtracking, they'd spot it for sure, maybe get a good shot, maybe not. But if, as both pilot and copilot suspected, the driver of the 450 was playing it cagy, skulking just out of sight, waiting for them to come buzzing around the corner to investigate . . . then they were going to have better than a hundred-meter straight run from behind on a stationary target that couldn't possibly break right or left to spoil their aim. *Gotcha*.

They edged out two blocks behind where they estimated their prey was sitting, just far enough to peer around a corner of a nine-story building and confirm that, yes, indeed, the duck was sitting there waiting for them, fat and green and juicy and *dead*. And then they whipped around and streaked forward, not ten meters off the pavement, right up the center line of the unmoving vehicle. The pilot had his finger on the firing button, but held back, waiting, waiting, like a man choking back orgasm to prolong that eye-popping anticipation. . . .

And behind a blown-out window in the second story of a building at the end of that first block of the run-in stood Billy McKay, feet braced wide, machine gun leveled, buttstock clamped with his elbow between hip and shortribs. As the helicopter whined into his field of vision from the left he pressed the trigger, fought to hold the muzzle down, and the helicopter flew right through the stream of copper-jacketed slugs.

The bullets were still going fast enough after they had chopped the copilot to hamburger to poke right on through the pilot and churn his soft vulnerable internal parts to mush. The pilot was still conscious, but he couldn't control his limbs, couldn't control the agile craft that was his limbs' extension. And so the chopper rolled gracefully to the left and just nosed into a building as if merely dropping in for a friendly visit. Flaming oil and grease and boiling blood dripped down into what had once been a Wendy's, and that was most definitely that.

They stopped at a nameless stucco suburb on the Kansas side of the line. It was starting to rain again. "This is where you get off, Dexter," Billy McKay said. "It's been real." He opened the side hatch and jumped down to the cracked asphalt of a Big O tire store parking lot.

Looking at the hulking ex-marine in distaste, White stepped down, ignoring the hand held out to help him. Jeff MacGregor came out behind him.

"Dex—" he said.

White turned to face him. "No, I won't shake your hand. I cannot condone the crimes you've committed today—allowed to be committed in your name—all in the service of your personal ambitions and selfish drives—"

He got no further. President of the United States Jeffrey MacGregor cocked a fist, hauled off, and hit him in the nose. He sat down smack on his broad bottom.

"You know, Billy," MacGregor said, trying not to massage his throbbing knuckles too overtly, "I've never done that to anyone before. Not ever." He looked down at White, and there was something in his gaze of the way a person would look at a piece of furniture, a discarded toaster perhaps. "It felt good."

McKay gave him a hand up into the vehicle. "You know, Jeff? You're all right." The door slammed. Mobile One purred away, leaving the Mayor of Kansas City sitting in his suit in the drizzle staring after them as they drove into the west.

Within a few blocks of taking their leave from Mayor White they started picking up Callahan's people. They paused to wait for Eklund's truck in a little shopping center mall next to a half-completed highway interchange.

"Oh well," Sam Sloan remarked as they crept westward, paralleling I-40, "at least we have a reasonably straight shot at the next candidate on our list." It was a good thing. Western Kansas, thickly sown with Minuteman launch sites and, since the first term of President William Lowell, MX missile silos as well, had taken a truly hellacious pounding during the War. Most of the warheads dropped in this area had targeted areas away from population centers—which left a whole lot of people in shape to get their cars stuck in immense traffic jams trying to escape the fallout. I-40 was nowhere very good; some traveler they talked to by a roadside campfire better than half a year and thousands of klicks away had aptly described it as a "continent-spanning traffic jam." Here, down the prevailing winds from Wichita and the craters of several groundbursts, even the normally little-used county roads, on which the Guardians so frequently relied, were choked with cars long dead.

All during that day the Guardians found themselves casting periodic nervous glances at the glum overcast sky. They weren't particularly concerned about pursuit by White's people. The Mayor frankly didn't have the resources to pursue any kind of personal vendetta with them once they left his fair city. But the encounter with the helicopter had reminded them that the FSE expeditionary force possessed a certain amount of air capability. Which made the possibility they'd be hunted by air a very real one.

The prospect wasn't especially reassuring. An armored car,

a panel truck, and a gaggle of motorcycles slugging across country was rare meat for aircraft. Especially when even the road's shoulders were too jammed to negotiate, and they were reduced to crawling alongside, Mobile One's treads tearing out great gouts of black wet soil held together in clumps by prairie grass roots. And this was Kansas into the bargain, which meant it didn't offer just a whole hell of a lot of interesting terrain features you could hide behind, under, or in.

They drove with hatches popped to the muggy air, watching the overcast skies and the land around. Sunlight had begun to slant in under the clouds at an oblique angle when they finally encountered other traffic.

CHAPTER
THIRTEEN ───────

It was a wagon, approaching from the south along a track that consisted of nothing more than a couple of ruts worn in the prairie. It had tires scrounged from cars, but it was still a real old-fashioned *wagon*, with a wooden bed and a raised box up front, four horses harnessed in two pairs. Even for a year after the fall of civilization as they knew it, the scene struck the Guardians as a little surreal: the older man with the reins in sun-hardened hands, wearing faded blue overalls and a battered straw hat; the younger man in torn jeans and grease-stained work shirt open over a white T-shirt lounging beside him in the box, smoking a cigarette. The only thing that spoiled the total Grant Wood *fin de siècle* nostalgic quality of it all was the long black Belgian FN-LAR the young man held negligently in one hand by the pistol grip.

At the sight of Callahan's riders the old man stopped the wagon and the young man slowly sat up, carefully cradling the assault rifle across his knees. It seemed to reassure them when they saw the armored car. A Super Commando could do more damage than a lot more bikers than this, but the two farmers seemed to believe that anyone who owned an armored car had to be a more reliable customer than motorcycle outlaws.

"Sam?" MacGregor said. "Could you pull over, please?"

"What's that, sir?"

"Pull over, if you would, please. I'd like to talk to these people."

"McKay? What do you think?"

"Do like the man said. It don't look like these people bite."

"They're looking a little nervous, Billy," Casey reported from the open turret.

"Point your guns somewhere else."

"Oh. Good point." The servos whirred briefly. The armored car came to a stop on the shoulder of the road not quite at the spot the wagon would cross the terminally congested highway. Sam Sloan boosted himself up so that his elbows rested on the rim of his hatch. "Afternoon," he called cheerily.

The wagon halted. The lead horses put their heads down instantly and began to pull up mouthfuls of the soft wet grass, switching their tails at flies that buzzed in profusion, indicating it was about to start raining again. "Good afternoon," the older man said. His voice, like the expression on his seamed and weathered old face, was carefully neutral, neither friendly nor hostile. The younger man was seriously trying not to fidget. The FN lay across his knees, and he didn't quite touch it, as if to say, "Why, this? _I_ don't have any idea how it came to be lying here."

"Mind if we talk a bit?" Sam Sloan asked.

A smile cracked the hardpan features. "You want to talk, reckon we can listen. Be only neighborly."

The side hatch opened and McKay stepped out, unarmed except for his sidearm. Jeff MacGregor stepped down next to him. Together they walked around the front of the car and down towards the wagon. "Good afternoon, gentlemen," MacGregor said. "I'm Jeff MacGregor. I'd like to have a few words with you, if you don't mind."

The younger man looked nervously at the older. The older man shrugged. "Don't mind. Wanted to make it up to Maitland by nightfall. But I reckon we could sit for a spell."

Sergeant Eklund's truck had pulled to a stop behind Mobile One. "Maybe we could go up and sit next to the truck, in case it starts to rain again," McKay said. "You could just leave your wagon here if your, ah, horses will be okay. Nobody's going to bother it.''

The oldster cast a glance at Mobile One, sitting up on the road like a huge metal toad. "Nope. Reckon nobody will."

The two of them jumped down from the box. After a moment's hesitation, the young man brought his FN with him. Sam's face looked a little nervous, hovering over the 450's front deck, but McKay wasn't particularly concerned. After taking on a heavily armed platoon and a helicopter already that day, he wasn't in any frame of mind to be too uptight over some hayseed with a 7.62 Belgian stick. Besides, he couldn't conceive that the young man could be carrying enough of a hard-on for Jeff MacGregor to make a play for him with ten tons of serious death sitting near enough to spit on.

"Pleased to meet you, Mr. MacGregor," the older man said as they walked up the slight grassy incline. "This here is my nephew, Jake. My name's Warren." He frowned slightly. "MacGregor, MacGregor. Name sounds familiar, somehow."

"I know him, Uncle Skeeter. He's some kind of actor. I seen him on the TV."

MacGregor laughed. McKay scowled. "What he is, is the President of the United States, Junior."

Uncle Skeeter put back his head and laughed a braying laugh. "And I'm the Queen of England."

"Now, listen, you crusty old—''

"Take it easy, Billy. It's okay. Mr. Warren—ah, Jake—this is Lieutenant William McKay. He's the commander of the Guardians."

"A pleasure, Mr. McKay."

"Yeah."

India Three was deassing the deuce-and-half to stretch their legs and get away from the smell of each other. They looked at the two farmers curiously. The two stared back, Jake nervously fingering his rifle. McKay introduced them to Sergeant Eklund, and didn't at all like the way Jake eyed her impressive frontage. "Got anything to offer our guests?" McKay asked.

Without turning around Eklund said, "Chi? How about some of that booze you liberated from the commissary."

"Ah, shit, Sergeant, you wasn't supposed to know about that." The lean trooper climbed back into the vehicle, emerged an instant later with a bottle of Jack Daniel's.

They all sat down in the shade of the truck. "So, what's on your mind—Mr. President?" The old fart cracked a hint of a smile, took a long draw from the bottle, wiped his mouth with the back of his hand, and passed it on.

MacGregor took a token swig. "I was just curious as to what you were doing in this area. It was pretty well devastated a year ago."

"Yep."

"So what brings you here now?"

"We live here," Jake said. "Got a farm a few—that is, a ways away from here." He obviously didn't trust the strangers completely as yet. McKay wasn't too surprised. This last year hadn't been a good one for trusting souls.

MacGregor looked disbelieving. "A farm? But what—what about the radiation?"

"Naw," Jake said. "Ain't much of that left. We got us a good Geiger counter, one of these little solar-powered jobbies from the mail order. That helps us keep clear of the hot spots."

"The worst stuff decays real fast, Mr. President," Cato offered. The two locals looked at him very intently when he used the word *president*. "That's what made it such a crock of shit back before the War when the people were always talking about these terrible isotopes with a half-life of a hundred eighty thousand years. Shit like that is barely radioactive at all. It's the stuff that decays real quick that kills you. And there's not much of that left, except in areas where the fallout is really concentrated."

"But I understood it *was* concentrated around here," MacGregor said. "That there were all the groundbursts on the missile farms and those Strategic Air Command bases near Wichita. And what about the bone-seekers—strontium-90, cesium-137? Those have a pretty long half-life. They can get inside you from your food and decay into more radioactive substances."

"Know all about 'em, Mr. MacGregor," Uncle Skeeter said calmly. "Mostly they stick close to the surface. If you scrape off the top layer of soil before you plow, you can get rid of most of 'em.''

"Ain't that a lot of work, man?" Rosie asked.

"Shit, yes!" Jake laughed.

MacGregor shook his head, remembering the nuclear-disaster movies of the 1980s—the terrible apathy, the look of bone-deep desperation as some representative of the government explained to a group of half-starved farmers that they'd have to clear the topsoil from their acreage before they could plant it, for fear of bone-seekers. Now these two were talking matter-of-factly about doing just that. "But that—you can't possibly filter out all of the bone-seekers. Some of it's going to get into your crops, into your animals. Isn't that dangerous?"

Uncle Skeeter took another swig of Evil Jack, swished it around his mouth. "Ain't half so dangerous as starving."

"But the risk of cancer—"

"Now, Mr. MacGregor, maybe you are the President of the United States, and if you are, more power to you. But what you're doing hunkered by the side of some Kansas road with a couple of sodbusters is beyond me. And I don't mean no disrespect, but what makes you think life ought to be easy? Ain't never been for farmers. Probably not for most people. Now less than ever.

"So it's a royal pain in the—pardon me, ma'am—that we gotta scrape off the top layer of soil before we can plow, and all the time be scouting our grazing land with a Geiger counter. No, we know there's no way we're going to get all that radioactive stuff out. And so maybe some of us'll get the leukemia or something—twenty, thirty year down the line. If something else don't kill us off first. And so what? Son, I mebbe learned just one thing in life, and that's that no one leaves this world alive. And in the meantime we just do the best we can, and thank the good Lord above for the chance."

The day had gotten late and the ground hadn't gotten any firmer. The occupants of the two vehicles and Callahan's Desperadoes decided to laager down for the night. The farmers were induced to stay over. Because this part of the world really had been an annex of hell a short year before, not too many people from the outside world got through here. The pair were eager to learn what was going on in the rest of the United States—and the protection offered by Mobile One's awesome armament against any chance raiders encouraged them greatly.

"Them New Dispensation sonsabitches get up here from time to time," said old Skeeter Warren round a mouthful of beans. "Body can't be too careful."

They squatted around a fire of the driest grass and brush they could find, primed with gas siphoned from the tanks of stalled vehicles and burning in a cut-down fifty-five gallon oil drum. It made a pretty smoky and unsatisfactory fire, but really all they were looking for was a little light, a little warmth, a focus for nighttime camaraderie. Ragged clouds and swatches of clear black starshot sky were chasing each other overhead, the moon veering crazily in and out of cover; in case it rained again, they had rigged a sort of lean-to out of a tarp dogged to the trailer of a Safeway semi. The field crickets were going at it full volume, and from away off far came the trill of a bullfrog, an eeerie yet pleasant sound to McKay's city ears.

"They're why we come up here to start with," Jake said. "To get away from them nuts."

His uncle nodded enthusiastically. "We're believing Christian folk. Most of the folks as settled around here are. And me and my wife Lisa Beth, we used to listen to Reverend Forrie on the radio all the time. Lived somewhere in northern Oklahoma those days, don't matter where no more. Then come the War, and the cholera took Lisa Beth, and that Coffin fella showed up. A lot of folk thought he was touched by God himself, but I always thought he was as crazy as a bedbug myself. And the people who heard him, danged if they didn't start acting crazy too. And they started joining up with this Crusade of his, good folks, solid working people. Them that din't—well sir, they always had to keep an eye on what they said, or they might find themselves being visited in the middle of the night by the Brothers of Mercy." He shook his head and spit into the fire. "And then we found out old man Coffin had hooked up with a bunch of them road gypsy fellas."

"Scum," young Jake said. His eyes burned with a light that didn't seem altogether reflected.

The old man bared his teeth in something that wasn't a

smile. "Jake, here," he said quietly, "lost his sister Ellie to those boys. Caught her out for a horseback ride with her beau, Jordy. Killed him with a chainsaw, they did. And Ellie—" He shook his head, eyeing Eklund sidelong. He still hadn't quite adjusted to the presence of a lady sergeant. It cramped his narrative style. "They—they used her, you know? Busted her up inside, so bad she died. Jake's dad tried to get the local sheriff after them, and we never see him again. Seemed they was in real tight with this *Reverend* Coffin."

McKay smiled. "We've had one or two run-ins with the road gypsies."

"I hope you killed lots of them," Jake said fervently.

The smile broadened. "We did."

Feeling the need to stretch his legs, sometime after dinner, McKay took his machine gun and wandered off to stand by a culvert where a little stream ran rapid under the road. Frogs dived into the water with little plopping sounds as he came up and perched his butt on a tire rim stuck halfway in the mud. He sat dropping pebbles in the water, thinking of nothing in particular.

After a while Marla appeared next to him. He had to admire the quiet way she moved for all her size. It reminded him of himself. She'd bathed discreetly around a bend in the stream this afternoon while they were talking with Skeeter and Jake, after it had been decided to stay there the night, and now smelled of sweet scavenged soap.

She leaned forward, kissed him on his cheekful of evening bristle. Then she sat down and stared at the star-images rippling on the surface of the water. "We're pulling out tomorrow."

He just sat there nodding his head. "Where you going?"

"We don't know yet. Maybe back to Luxor to see how Gillet is doing. Maybe hook up with some Army outfit that isn't lousy with Effsees. Maybe just hire on with some townsfolk who could use a hand dealing with road gypsies and such." She smiled, not too steadily. "Maybe the people over to Maitland could use us." Maitland, it turned out, was a settlement that had sprung up since the War, as people began to drift back into what had been a radioactive dead zone, driven

by hunger or ambition or intolerable situations to become the
new pioneers, recolonizing America's heartland.

"Big-time mercenaries, huh?" McKay said.

"Maybe they'll make me foldout of the month in *Soldier of
Fortune*."

McKay laughed sourly. They sat for a while in silence, and
all the time he was becoming more and more aware of her.
Maybe more than he'd ever been. Finally he grunted and said,
"Okay. I'll bite. *Why?*"

"You-all've always got to move fast to get the President to
where he's got to go, wherever that is. If this hombre Maximov didn't know you got Jeff out of Heartland before, he
does now for sure. We can't really keep up. And after what
happened in KC"—she shook her head, blinking quickly, and
her voice took on an edge—"we ain't trained for this kind of
thing. You know what we are—a scratch platoon. Buncha
refugees and survivors I scraped together myself. Not even a
line unit."

"Your people've been a lot of help to us."

"We did what we could and died a lot. And that's fine. But
Kansas City proved something to me. You boys—you and
Sammy and Casey and Tom—you operate as a team. Just the
way you should. And we ain't nowhere as good, and for all the
time we spent together we can't fit in with you that smooth.
We just get in your way. And you keep getting stuck into
situations that get us killed off." Her breath came ragged, like
a fraying hem of cloth.

"Now, wait a minute, we never—"

She touched her finger to his lips. "No. I ain't accusing you
of throwing our lives away. It's just that we can't possibly survive in the—oh, shit, what do they call it?—combat environ-
ment where you do. So we aren't doing you a whole hell of a
lot of good, and we're slowing you down, and all the time
we're dying off." She shook her head. "And I—maybe I ain't
tough enough. I just can't take it anymore."

Feeling awkward, he put his arm around her. He could have
told her she was just as tough as they came. That she was as
good a troop as he'd ever worked with. And it would have
been true.

But he didn't.

Because she was right. The kind of operations the Guardians engaged in, extra bodies just tended to be extra targets. India Three had saved their asses on a couple of occasions—and India Three had also taken better than fifty percent fatalities since they'd hooked up together in the terrible spring of that year. McKay was willing to sacrifice anything and anybody to the mission, including himself and his three comrades. But it was a whole hell of a lot easier to throw away the lives of people you hardly knew.

Then there was Marla herself.

"Good luck," he said. She turned to him, and put her mouth to his, and for a while everything was fine.

CHAPTER
FOURTEEN ——————————

The morning was so bright and clear it ached like a hollow tooth. Jake and Uncle Skeeter got on their way after breakfast shared with the soldiers and with Callahan's bikers, whom they regarded with wary skepticism. The bikers had mainly kept to themselves; the ill feelings with which they had parted outside Kansas City hadn't been entirely counterfeit.

McKay hadn't told anyone else about Eklund's intentions. Nonetheless, it was as if everyone realized that the group would be splitting up soon. Breakfast was subdued, with India Three and the Guardians just kind of naturally hanging in two separate lumps, and Eklund and McKay avoiding each other's eyes.

By 10:00 A.M. they had reached the interchange of I-70 and I-135, just north of the town of Salina. By prior arrangement with Eklund, McKay called a halt. The others in Mobile One looked at him curiously as he opened the side door and jumped down to the gravel of the shoulder. "C'mon out, everybody," he called back into the car. "We got some goodbyes to say."

Puzzled and blinking, MacGregor and the other three Guardians emerged into the hot morning air. Sunlight spar-

kled off the cars that completely covered the Christmas-
package bow of the interchange. Windshields, mostly still intact, sent back hard eye-hurting glints of sun. The air smelled
of green and rust.

India Three's truck came groaning and protesting on the
soft soil incline of the roadbed, heeling dangerously over to
the right. Tall Bear drove, Eklund rode next to him. "We'll be
going north, into Nebraska," the Kiowa corporal said.

"Then where?" McKay asked. His companions were looking from him to the corporal, curious.

Tall Bear shrugged. "Who knows? Sergeant'll think of
something. She always does."

India Three opened the Mercedes' rear gates and climbed
out. "What's going on, Billy?" Casey asked.

"These folks're going their own way." Casey and Sam and
the President looked sad, taken aback. Rogers's face showed
little emotion, as usual, but McKay had the distinct feeling
that he was relieved.

And so they each said good-bye, with a few words and a
smile or just a nod and a handshake: Rosie, Cato, Sandy, little
Torrance, so quiet you hardly knew she was there, Nguyen,
Chi, giant Jamake. Sandy got teary-eyed and hugged and
kissed each of them, even the President. The Desperadoes hovered off in the shade of the interchange itself, engines idling in
a soft growl, but Callahan came stumping back to shake hands
with the departing platoon as well. His crew would be accom-
panying the Guardians to their own base in Colorado.

Like a dark stocky cloud Corporal Tall Bear stumped from
one to the other, shaking hands in glum silence. "Been a pleasure serving with you, Corporal," Sam Sloan said, when his
turn came.

"Wish I could say the same."

McKay's face reddened. He stepped toward the Indian. "At
ease, McKay," Sam said. Tall Bear's heavy face remained
impassive as always, but in those earth-brown eyes Sam had
caught a hint of the corporal's pain. Association with the
Guardians had killed over half of India Three; unlike Eklund,
Tall Bear blamed the Guardians.

Last of all came Sergeant Marla Eklund. She gave each man
a kiss and a handshake, until she came to McKay.

He tried to fend her off. "Look, lady, I come from a long line of Marines. If they found out I got caught kissing a sergeant in public—" But she grabbed him with that astonishing weightlifter's strength of hers, crushed her mouth to his, kissed him good and hard and long, not caring if this was public or not. He gave up and kissed her back. When they broke apart she hugged him so hard that even his massive ribs creaked. She put her cheek to his.

"I love you," she said.

He just stared past her, out at the green flatland, and hugged her tightly.

After a moment, she broke away and walked away from him, her boots crunching on gravel. At the side of the truck she stopped, barked an order for the platoon to form a line. With surprising smartness they did so. As one they snapped off a salute to their comrades in arms, the Guardians and the President of the United States. The Guardians snapped to attention and saluted back.

Then the squaddies bundled back into their vehicle. Tall Bear fired it up and off they went. As they rattled north along 135 toward Nebraska, Chitown called out over the tailgate, "Hang loose, bro's." And he held his fist up and waggled it, little finger and thumb extended, and that was the last they saw of India Three.

"No way," Ruby Vasquez said. The diminutive redheaded Chicano sat with her legs drawn up beneath her in a heavy butcher-block chair in Angie Connoly's living room. She took another puff on her long black cigarillo—she smoked the same brand as Callahan. "There is just no way you are going to use the Denver Federal Center."

McKay stuck out his chin. "How do you know so much about it?" he challenged.

Ruby laughed. McKay's frown deepened. He was just breaking wind and he knew it. If the foxy little physician ever said things she couldn't back up, she hadn't yet done it in McKay's hearing. Physically the tiny, dark Vasquez and blond, strapping Marla Eklund couldn't have been further apart; down inside they bore similarities that were making McKay decidedly uncomfortable.

Cool mountain air whispered through the low-beamed living room, helped along by the subtlest assistance of small fans running off solar-power accumulators. The Connoly house, like most in the libertarian settlement called Freehold, was semisubterranean, mostly below ground level and covered by thick insulating layers of earth. You'd hardly ever know it, though, the way the clerestory and the skylights opened the top up to a sky that simply exploded with stars, and the way the south-facing picture windows looked out over the San Luis Valley, a gentle greenish silver expanse in the light of half a moon.

"We've got a lot of contacts with people in the Denver rubble now, and some of us do scavenger work ourselves." Their hostess, Angie Connoly, sat on a low sofa with her back against a priceless black-on-gray Navajo rug. Casey Wilson slouched happily at her side. She was a tall woman, at five feet ten only an inch shorter than Casey himself, with chiseled features and striking blue eyes and hair so black it was almost blue. The last time they'd been here it had hung almost down to her rump. Now it was bobbed close, if nowhere near Eklund's military crew cut. A knobby cane of some black hardwood was propped discreetly against the end of the sofa near her right hand. Since the Guardians' last visit weeks ago, during preparations for the assault on Heartland, she had been shot in the left thigh in a skirmish with the Freehold's neighbors, the Northern Rio Grande Valley Association. Though Angie Connoly's politics struck McKay as frankly crazy, her injury did nothing to make him sorry that they'd had to deal strongly with some NRGVA types on the way in. Served the dumb fucks right for tangling with an armored car, anyway.

The four Guardians and Dreadlock Callahan had arrived two hours before, shortly after sunset, having been only slightly delayed by the encounter. The NRGVA had been besieging the Freehold with some seriousness at the behest of William Lowell's government and his friends the FSE. Now some time had passed since anything had been heard from old Wild Bill, and the FSE expeditionary force was obviously suffering a severe crisis of command, so the Association had decided to slack off on their neighbors somewhat. Going with the flow had always been one of the hallmarks of that splendid organization.

"If you can lend us the personnel," Sam Sloan said, "I think we could evict any unwanted tenants from the Center. Probably without the need to resort to too much violence."

Ruby and Angie exchanged looks. "First of all," Angie said, "we can't 'lend' anyone to you. If anyone wants to go with you, they'll go; if they don't, they won't."

"And nobody will," Ruby said.

They looked at her in consternation. "You boys have been allowing yourselves to be misled by the fact that we've had a good working relationship since the War," she went on. She gave McKay a lascivious smirk. "Better than that, in a couple cases I could name. Some of us are sympathetic to you personally—and some of us aren't. And there are debts between us. But I think I can safely speak for all the Freeholders—and this may be the only point in the whole wide world I could do that—when I tell you that nobody is going to be willing to risk her damn neck to restore the government of the United States."

McKay felt his neck growing warm. "But it's your patriotic duty—"

Ruby slammed her palm down on the arm of her chair. "*Fuck* duty!"

"Mr. McKay," Angie put in, more calmly but forcefully still, "the stewardship of the United States Government has brought about the deaths of what our best figures indicate are upwards of three quarters of the American population. At that, you're doing better than the Soviets; what we can glean, largely by tapping in on Chairman Maximov's communication satellites, indicates Russia's population is down to fifteen percent of pre-War totals. But I think these facts more than deal with any lingering doubts we had about government serving the people."

"But this is the President of the United States we're talking about here," said Sam, leaning forward earnestly with hands on knees. "Don't you think you owe him something?"

Ruby took a puff on her cigarette, squinted at Sloan, and blew her smoke. "Why? None of us voted for him. Besides, no American owes either loyalty or obedience to the President of the United States. Check your Constitution, son."

Sam blinked at being addressed as "son" by a woman not more than a decade his senior, and who could have passed for his own age. But Jeff MacGregor nodded. "She's right, Sam. The American people are the sovereign; as President, I'm their representative. These people don't seem inclined to accept me as *their* representative. Altogether, I can't wholly blame them."

"But this country needs a strong government, dammit—" McKay said.

"Wild Bill and the Effsees gave us a strong government," Ruby said. "Strong on the order of Stalin in Russia, or Pol Pot in Kampuchea. And you sat in this very living room plotting how to overthrow that government, and the fact that you are sitting here again with all your parts and with Jeff MacGregor in tow proves you succeeded. So what's this 'strong government' shit?"

The conference was clearly developing into a confrontation between two armed camps, with Dreadlock Callahan sitting off to one side in a spotless white jumpsuit—God alone knew where he got it—looking amused. And even Casey and Angie had sidled a few centimeters away from one another on the sofa and sat with muscles tensed, as if ready to spring apart.

Jeff MacGregor held his hands in the air. "Peace, people. We've got no reason to fight among ourselves." Everybody looked at him. "I'm new to your community, Ms. Connoly, Dr. Vasquez. But from the reports the Guardians brought back I feel I know it very well. Despite your philosophical differences with us, you have offered us a great deal of invaluable help in the past." He paused, grinned. "And it might not be inappropriate to remind you of the assistance the Guardians have tendered *you*."

"We do appreciate the debts we owe the Guardians, Mr. MacGregor," Angie said. She seemed to have unwound a few notches.

Ruby Vasquez uttered a sharp bark of laughter. "So we're all speaking a little out of turn. And it's all just pissing in the wind anyway. Because if you got every woman, man, and child above the age of six to line up like good little draftees and march north on the Denver Federal Center, it wouldn't do one damn bit of good. DFC's swarming with the New Dispensation like a corpse with maggots. They have that place locked in tight. It would take an army to bust in there—a lot bigger, better army than a handful of anarchists and four boy heroes in a tin-plated Toyota." She sipped smoke from her cigar, blew three rings. "So if you want to go up there and get your asses shot off, feel free; some of us will feel bad. But none of us will lift a finger to help you."

McKay was starting to cloud over again. She squirted a stream of smoke straight at his big angry face. "But I imagine we could scare up a couple of people to guide you in there, just to show you exactly the kind of fool's errand you are proposing here."

McKay scowled at her a moment longer. And then he laughed. "You're on."

The party broke up. Dreadlock Callahan excused himself as graciously as a viscount, kissing Angie Connoly's hand in parting—McKay never *could* read that dude. Ruby Vasquez grabbed McKay's sleeve. "Time for bed, big boy." He still had some very pissed-off undercurrents flowing in her direction; he knew better than to try to fight them. The very fundamental antagonism between his outlook and Ruby Vasquez's they took out on each other in bed, and both of them liked it. A night with the redheaded Chicana was always an experience; maybe it would help get Marla out of his mind.

Angie Connoly and Casey were standing hand in hand. For Sloan, who'd never been able to connect with any of the Freehold women, there was a guest bedroom and solitude, for what that was worth. Tom Rogers preferred to sleep in the truck. He hadn't connected either, not with any woman any of his buddies knew about in the year since the War. He did not seem prey to most of the weaknesses the flesh was heir to. By now his comrades were used to thinking of the ex-Green Beret as being more an elemental force of nature than a man.

"Let's get a move on, then," grumbled Billy McKay. "I got to get *some* sleep."

"Holy shit," Billy McKay said.

He and Tom Rogers and this skinny Chicano kid named Manuel, who had a red rag tied around his head and looked to be about four feet tall, were hunched down in the ruins of the planetarium across from the Federal Center. When they'd been by here a year ago, the planetarium had been intact. Now it was busted open and burned out, everything inside smashed, trashed, and bashed. One of the New Dispensation's credos was a frothing hatred of technology—except when it was being used to further the ends of the Church.

The Denver Federal Center was just chock-full of technology that might further those ends. It was also full of the faithful. A steady stream of trucks, wagons, and foot traffic poured in and out between the stone watchtowers at the gate through the three-meter wire fence. Aside from the machine guns mounted in the towers, McKay could see at least a squad of black-clad Brothers of Mercy, the Church's shock troops, several of whom sported the Mohawks and other outlandish hairstyles and general accoutrements of road gypsies. They were all armed with automatic weapons, and just in the area of the gate McKay counted four different antitank rocket launchers in plain view, each of a different type.

Beyond the fence, the rolling parklike expanse of the Center was thronged. Apparently the predominantly subterranean facilities were full, or at least declared off-limits to the grunts. A tent city of sorts occupied much of the grounds, a colorful forest of everything from one-man shelters to a pavilion that had once housed the Kingfish County Fair bingo game. Several hectares surrounding the aboveground structures had been trampled down to yellow mud by thousands upon thousands of feet. Nearby, twenty or thirty faithful armed with rifles practiced advancing by short rushes and throwing themselves face first on the ground under the watchful eye of the drill instructor in black leather with his hair waxed up into a single magenta spike jutting from the top of his head.

"They're all over the place," the boy whispered in McKay's ear. "If we hadn't snuck here before dawn, we wouldn't never made it here. Even," he added, "though you nearly quiet as me."

McKay stifled the urge to cuff the little bastard. He had to admit the kid had stolen overland from the shopping center where they had stashed Sam, Casey, and Dr. Vasquez in the V-450 with no more noise than a flitting shadow. And he'd picked the best spot to hide out; the New Dispensation types seemed to avoid the planetarium like the plague. *Probably some kind of taboo*, he thought.

"Looks bad, Billy," Rogers said.

"No shit." He peered through binoculars at the gate. A spikes-and-leather guard displaying the mushroom hairlessness and corpse pallor of a zombi addict stood holding a full-dress M-60 while a stubby potbellied little fuck in a baseball cap—who looked for all the world like a truck driver, and probably was—gave each incoming vehicle a quick once-over before waving it in. The New Dispensation made some pretty damn strange bedfellows.

As security arrangements go, it wasn't much; McKay figured he could get himself and the Guardians and probably Dreadlock's people in here without half a problem, lying under cargo in the bed of a few trucks. . . . He shook his head. He was daydreaming. This wasn't any snatch-and-grab or straight sabotage mission. He was fairly certain they could pull off one of those, no sweat. What they could not do was take and hold the citadel, not unless, say, what remained of the FSE expeditionary force agreed to lend a hand. The bad guys had guns and cadre and, unless his eyes deceived him, a couple of sandbagged mortar emplacements among the brick and masonry buildings. More than that, he knew full well that even the humblest and feeblest among the faithful would fight like a rabid badger to defend his church.

He lowered the glasses. Something caught his eye, ten or twenty meters to the south of the gate. An X of wooden railroad ties, blackened, with something attached to it—looked like a monkey or a little black doll. *What the fuck?*

"What's that?" he asked, focusing his glasses on the thing.

Beside him he could actually *feel* the skinny Mexican kid coil up into a tight quivering ball of hatred and anger. "My cousin Louie," the boy said, his voice trembling like a leaf in windstorm. "They caught him trying to sneak in."

McKay caught a blur, fiddled with the focus. And suddenly it leapt out at him: a tiny twisted charcoal figure, grinning at him with shocking white teeth, and showing through the crust of blackness here and there a hint of more bone white. "They set him up there and sprayed gasoline on him," the boy said.

"But he was a real man; he didn't scream until they lit him."

"Jesus fucking *Christ*," McKay said.

"What say, Billy?" Casey's voice said in his ear. Mobile One was stashed less than a klick away. It was a temptation to call for it to come up and blow a few hundred assholes into hamburger. But McKay knew what that would accomplish, which was precisely nothing. He already knew they couldn't save the world or even any sizable chunk of it. Right now they had the President to take care of, and they wouldn't accomplish that by letting some asshole with a shaven head and a gold ring in his ear blow Mobile One into spare parts with a LAW.

"Nothing, Case." No point in ruining his day. Which he was about to do, anyway. "But Denver Federal Center is right straight fucking out. I say again, DFC is a definite no go."

"I told you so," Ruby Vasquez said, cutting herself in by way of hand mike.

"Isn't there anything you can do, McKay?" Sloan asked.

"What we need is an entire goddamned wing of Phantoms loaded with napalm." He glanced again at the black effigy twisted against the blue Rocky Mountain sky. "Come to think of it, that's just what these assholes need, too."

They were in Arizona when the call came through.

None of them had very good feelings about California anymore, but it was a bet they had to check out. The Freeholders had contacts on the West Coast, and what filtered back through their network was universally bad. There were a lot of Effsees out there, and they were very firmly in control of some of the most desirable real estate—including New Eden. Nonetheless, it still looked like their best bet for a safe haven for the President.

They were traveling light. Dreadlock and his Desperadoes had been left behind at the Freehold, to go back to pulling security on Freeholder trade convoys. McKay reckoned the other Guardians felt just about the way he did about it: relieved. The Desperadoes had been invaluable allies. They had unquestionably hauled the Guardians' fat out of the fire in Kansas City, admittedly with a little help from one William

Kosciusko McKay. But they were very chancy allies, skittish, combative, and none too reliable. With the possible exception of Dreadlock Callahan—who was in a class by himself—none of them were the sort of people any of the Guardians would have chosen to hang around with. Except maybe the younger Billy McKay, the same specimen who would have tagged Sam Sloan as a typical Navy pussy, Casey Wilson as a fruitbar, and possibly even come up with something outrageous enough to sting the deceptively mild-seeming Tom Rogers into action— which, the mature McKay realized, would have been the worst and possibly the last mistake he could ever make.

They had swung southwest out of the San Luis Valley, clipping the northwest edge of New Mexico just below the Four Corners, angling down across Arizona in a transverse slash. Several times they'd spotted contrails bisecting the sky, once spotted the silver glint of a plane high up; the Effsees had been stirred up like a nestful of hornets and no mistake. Their magic open sesame into the expeditionary force communications net—the code keys they had found in Mobile One after capturing it from the Effsees—let them listen in and reassure themselves they'd hadn't been spotted by any of the overflights, but each man's throat went dry at every reminder of their enemies' power.

They were intending to round the mountains that walled Los Angeles off from the rest of the continent at their southern tip and cut back up into the vast ruined urban sprawl. The Effsees hadn't penetrated it to any great extent; a lot of scavengers—men and women plugged into Jake Morgenstern's trade network—had done so. It would provide their best bet for a secure base of operations until they could find a permanent home for the President.

So here they were flaked out beneath a sky that looked like something from a Juarez velvet painting, west of Phoenix between two mountain ranges in a patch of desert so dry and desperate not even Casey Wilson could find anything nice to say about it. Next morning they were going to push into California and get right up against it.

And then the radio spoke to them on a frequency no living person should have known.

Sam had been playing with the vehicle's radio, scanning the

freeks, listening to all the chatter that FSE thought was privileged. Or at least much of it; the really high-powered stuff, the high-command communications and the silver cord that linked the expeditionary force with the Federated States of Europe and its evil eminence across the Atlantic, used laser transmissions and satellite relays. Unless you could interrupt the pencil-thin beam or bug the satellite itself, there was no way to listen in. The Guardians had no hope of doing either, so they had to content themselves with the lower-level chatter.

Which was enlightening. The good news was that the expeditionary force was in a panic. Heartland's destruction seemed to have acted as a catalyst; instantly the morale of the invaders everywhere across the continent had sagged, and a thousand and one pockets of resistance, as if sensing this, burst like pustules into open rebellion. There was talk of battles in Wyoming, Ohio, Georgia. A strike at an Effsee-held uranium mine in western New Mexico, not many hundred klicks to the east. Confused reports of a raid by swampers in swamp boats against an FSE hovercraft patrol in eastern Florida. In Chicago, the densest concentration of expeditionary force troops the Guardians knew of, the rebels—some of whom had been organized and trained by Tom Rogers himself, during the months of fevered activity that lead up to the assault on Heartland—had pulled in confusion into the southern suburbs. And in Kansas City, where local commander Colonel Piet Derkszoon was recovering satisfactorily from severe burns on the lower half of his body, widespread rioting had broken out. Chief Peary's men and the shattered Expeditionary Force contingent were being hard pressed to contain it.

The bad news was that the Effsees knew the Guardians were on the loose with Jeff MacGregor, and everybody and his dog was hunting them across the length and breadth of America.

Another report on the Kansas City troubles came in. McKay plucked his cigar from his face and showed a wolf's grin to Sam Sloan. "The wave of the future, huh? Cooperation like you'd never seen before among Americans, huh?"

But Sloan only shook his head, his long face weary and sad in the blue instrument glow of his high-tech panel. "It meant a lot to us—and to the country—for Kansas City to be the place we were looking for. I guess I saw what I wanted to see." A quirky smile. "Wouldn't be the first time. Wish I could even hope it would be the last."

An annunciator buzzed. An orange eye began to blink on the console. "Call incoming on Guardian-restricted frequency," Sam Sloan remarked offhandedly, reaching for the keyboard. His hand halted with the fingers quivering a centimeter above the keys.

"What's going on here, Sam?" Casey Wilson's voice asked through the earphones. The former pilot was sitting in the lotus position atop the turret, enjoying the fresh desert air, practicing meditation, and incidentally keeping a very keen-eyed lookout in all directions. "Nobody's got those frequencies anymore. Not even the Effsees."

Inside the vehicle the other Guardians were looking at each other with stunned amazement. Even Jeff MacGregor, less intimately acquainted with the mechanical details of Guardians operations, looked perplexed. "Since the FSE doesn't know this frequency," Tom Rogers remarked, "maybe we should answer and find out who does."

Sloan shrugged. "They can't trace us if all we do is listen to their transmission." He looked at McKay. The burly ex-Marine nodded. Sloan hit the button.

"—calling Guardians. This is Balin's Forge calling the Guardians. Acknowledge please, Guardians. Over."

CHAPTER
FIFTEEN ──────────────

The message repeated itself while the Guardians gaped. The voice seemed to belong to a mature black male. Finally McKay shook himself. "What are you waiting for? Answer the man."

Sloan hesitated. "This could be a trap. They could be waiting to pinpoint us when we respond."

"So what? If they try to vector anybody in on us, we'll hear about it; even *I* know you can't keep operational control of troops via lasercast."

Sloan hit the transmit key. "Guardians acknowledging. Repeat, Guardians acknowledging. Come in, Balin's Forge. Come in, the Forge."

Snap, crackle, and pause. "This is the Forge, Guardians. I read you. Who am I talking to?"

"Commander Samuel Sloan."

"Oh so? What color are your shoes, Commander?"

Sam Sloan stared at the console in disbelief. *Is this guy out of his mind?* He realized McKay was grinning at him.

Suddenly he got it. During their stay at Balin's Forge, in the Simi Valley north of L.A., McKay had ribbed his comrade several times about being a blackshoe Navy officer. "Black. And who am I talking to?"

"Idaho. Same color as your shoes." They heard a chuckle.

McKay leaned forward. "And what's your relationship to Balin the Dwarf?"

"Huh? Why I'm his loyal friend and adviser—"

"Yeah, yeah. But before, what were you before?"

"So Jeannie told you, did she? I was Balin's parole officer."

"You're on, Idaho, my man. What's on your mind?"

"You dudes are bringing a very high-priority parcel this way, aren't you?" Sam Sloan looked from the console to McKay, and wondered if the Marine felt the same ball of ice forming in the pit of his gut that he did.

"Why, what makes you say that, Idaho?" he asked.

"No need to play coy, Sam. The Effsees' command net is full of it."

"The Effsees' command net is on laser. How do you know what's going over it?"

"We have our ways. You might remember that Silicon Valley isn't all that terribly far from here."

Sloan looked to McKay and nodded. Somebody in California had figured out how to get into the satellites orbiting changelessly overhead, electronically at least. One of the good guys—or so it seemed. "I read you five-by, Idaho. So what's the situation?"

"Anything but good. The expeditionary force has got Sacramento set up as their new North American headquarters. They're concentrating their strength in California. Got four or five thousand men here already, more coming in every day." It didn't sound like a lot of men, but the Guardians knew better. In present-day America, that many troops—trained, well equipped, with resupply, reliable communications, and coordinated command—was a force to be reckoned with. Given that Maximov's expeditionary force hadn't quite reached the twenty-thousand-man mark, it was almost certainly the major concentration of Effsee forces now. Not many men to hold the USA, or even the state of California, but still a lot more effective force than any other party could boast.

As witness the situation of the President of the United

States. At the moment *his* available forces consisted of four men and one armored car.

And the expeditionary force had some very useful allies. "They've got a General Price—American turncoat—running the show. Or at least the military angle. Where civilian matters are concerned he's got an 'adviser' who pulls the strings." Another chuckle. "An old friend of yours, I hear."

"The suspense is killing us," Sloan remarked dryly.

"Goes by the name of Ian Victor. British dude, or that's what he claims. You wouldn't believe what the rumor mill says he *really* is."

The Guardians looked at each other. Sam Sloan felt his lower jaw hanging slack in its muscles. McKay hit the transmit button with a stubby forefinger. "Oh yes we would."

"Ian Victor" was the *nom de guerre* of Colonel Ivan Vesensky, late of the KGB's Department V-for-Victor, the "wet affairs" bureau—the assassination department. He was also Yevgeny Maximov's most trusted—and most completely lethal —lieutenant. It had been Vesensky who pulled the strings of madcap Lieutenant Governor van Damm; falling afoul of the former lieutenant governor's rampant paranoia, the KGB traitor had been forced to flee for his life in the final hours before the climactic shootout between van Damm's crazy entourage and the Guardians in Disneyland.

"I hoped we'd seen the last of him," Sloan remarked, not transmitting.

"Guess again," McKay grunted.

"Now that we've got the society news out of the way," Idaho continued, "I have a personal message from the man who told us how to get in touch with you. A certain Dr. J."

"Dr. J?" Sloan asked, frowning. "J as in Jac—" Abruptly he shut up.

"J as in Jaybird," Idaho said smoothly.

"Jacob Morgenstern," Sam Sloan said, off the air. He punched the send button. "And what message does this Dr. J have for us?"

"He says he figures that with California denied to you, there's only one place you can take MacGregor. He says that it will be very risky. But he knows someone who could help you."

"Help us?"

"That's affirmative. Somebody in, uh, Albuquerque."

"Albuquerque?" McKay echoed. "Jesus Christ."

"How do we get in touch with this somebody?" Sloan asked.

"I'll give you a name, a frequency, and a time." He did so.

"Roger, Idaho, we've got it." Sloan grinned. "Tell Rhoda that Casey sends his love."

"Roger. The same on this end. Good luck to you dudes. Oh, and one more thing. When you get where you are going, if you find your asses stuck in a very tight crack, just look for the biggest, baddest nigger around and tell him Idaho sent you. Got that?"

"We copy, Balin's Forge. Thanks."

"You're welcome, Guardians. Good luck to you. Idaho out."

"Good luck to you, Idaho. Guardians out." Sloan shook his head. "Sounds like they need it at least as much as we do."

"I don't like to tell you gentlemen your business," MacGregor said, "but is there any possibility this could be a trap?"

"Not unless the Effsees have gotten so tricky they're outsmarting themselves," McKay said. "Would've been the easiest thing in the world to lure us right on into the Forge and jump us there. 'Stead of sending us back across two thirds of the continent."

MacGregor still looked puzzled. "You're all talking like it's all settled where we go next. Will somebody clue me in?"

Sam looked to McKay. "Our old friend Vesensky is a pretty shrewd sonofagun. If Dr. Morgenstern has figured out where we're going next, can we safely assume he hasn't, too?"

"Negative. We got to assume that he knows. And he's gonna throw everything he's got in front of us. That's why it's so important to see what kind of help we can get in Albuquerque."

"Where are we going?" MacGregor asked, almost plaintively.

Sloan grinned. "You've won, Mr. President. You and Billy McKay. We're going to Washington."

● ● ●

"I wonder when they're comin'?" Private Dowell squinted into the darkness, shifting his weight excitedly from boot to boot.

Standing watch at the gate cut into the wire on the western verge of the disused north-south runway, FSE expeditionary force trooper Raskob scowled at his comrade through thick wire-rimmed glasses. "Who the fuck knows? And will you fucking *calm down?*"

The old desert wind sighed and moaned around, making soft hints of hooting sounds through the burned-out shells of cars in the rental lot, through the civilian repair shops and hangar huddled across the road, and the looted, vacant airport buildings beyond that. "It just makes me nervous out here," Dowell said. "And it's that city out there. All dark and dead. I feel like, like—like there's something *there*, you know? Like something big and evil sleeping out there in all that dark and empty, and if we're out here long enough, it will wake up and come for us."

"Jesus Christ." Raskob shook his head, wagging the coal-scuttle helmet slightly on his red hair. "You been watching too many of them horror movies, you know?"

It *was* eerie out here, only he hated to admit it to that flake Dowell. He'd been stationed in Western Europe, which hadn't gotten nuked, and he never got into the German battle zone. He was used to riots, rebellion, reprisal bombing, and shelling reducing city hectares to rubble. What he wasn't used to was the proximity of a city that had been hit with a two-megaton hydrogen warhead.

Given the counterforce doctrine that both sides of necessity employed, the Soviets had shot primarily at missile farms and SAC bases. Few secondary targets had been hit. One which had was Albuquerque; its Kirtland Air Force Base was a major crossroads for transcontinental military air traffic. Since Soviet nuclear war-fighting doctrine rather optimistically called for prolonged conflict—the Soviet army offensive on the ground in Europe had actually begun to crap out inside a week, largely due to total logistic collapse—Kirtland had occupied considerable pride of place among the second-string targets, since it would be vital to America's continuing a conventional war. Of course, once the bombs fell, neither side had much interest in carrying on the conflict—neither side *existed*, in any meaningful sense. But the planners had had their way, and an SS-17 had popped its payload above the southeastern quadrant of the city, hypocenter several klicks north of the base. With the sheer klick-and-a-half face of the Sandia Mountains to reflect blast and flash onto the city, the single warhead had caused disproportionate destruction.

Though most of the base's complement had been killed, along with most of the rest of the population, a freak of over-pressure dynamics had meant that not only had a number of structures survived, but also a fair number of aircraft, usually the artifact most vulnerable to the effects of a nuclear blast. And the entire east-west runway remained usable, which meant that the missile had utterly failed at its task. As if that mattered now.

What mostly mattered now, to Raskob's mind, was that they had had their asses hauled out of comfortable bunks at Oh-dark-hundred on this early July morning to replace a couple of the sadsack survivors who passed for the local garrison on gate duty. An armored car full of Effsee special-duty troops was coming in, carrying some kind of civilian hotshot and the kind of priority clearance that makes you put God himself on hold. "I wonder what this is fucking all about, anyway," he said.

"Who knows? They never tell us legs nothing." A nervous glance northward along the cracked runway. "Like they don't tell us what's really out there. They try to keep it from us. But there's mutants out there, Fred. You can bet your life on it. Just watching . . . *waiting*."

"Mutants? *Mutants?* Just where in the *hell* did you get that?"

"I seen it in the movies, Fred. They're keeping it from us, hoping we don't find out. But I tell you, what that radiation does to a body—omigod!" He grabbed at Raskob's arm suddenly. The redhead reflexively danced away. Dowell jabbed the muzzle of his M-16 off to the right, along Yale Boulevard where it ran parallel to the abandoned runway. "Look!"

Raskob peered in that direction. Sure enough, a pair of

blackout headlights, coming their way. He unslung the Swedish Karl Gustav antitank rocket launcher from his shoulder, uncapped it, held it ready across his chest. They had yet to see an armored vehicle, indeed a military vehicle of any kind that wasn't expeditionary force. But they'd learned long ago what happened to soldiers of the Federated States who took unnecessary chances. He held his walkie-talkie close to his mouth. "Castle, this is Sleeping Beauty. Possible Prince Charming on the way."

Its diesel growling softly, the big car turned left onto the graveled expanse, which had once been a lookout for the curious to watch aircraft land and take off. The vehicle stopped amidst a grinding of pebbles under tires. The barrels of the two weapons in the turret were carefully averted, but they bespoke a great menace—at least to Raskob. He figured Dowell was too busy waiting for an army of the living dead to come lumbering out of the ruins and dismember them with chainsaws to fret himself about anything real.

A hatch popped in the turret, and a bullet-shaped, crew-cut head poked out, followed by one of the most massive sets of shoulders Raskob had ever seen on a human being. "All right," the head announced. "Here we are. You gonna open the gate, or just stand there poking your piles?"

Raskob's hands tensed hopefully on the grips of the Karl Gustav. It would be a lot of fun to rocket this goddamn car and watch this loudmouth sizzle. But the occupants of the car were Very Important People, and in the FSE, VIPs did what they goddamned well liked to grunts like Raskob. And to his partner, Dowell—who was still swiveling his eyes in all directions, looking for Pod People. "What's the password?" he barked, grateful for an official excuse to sound at least partially as pissed as he felt.

"Up your granny's ass, junior," the head said. "We're on Chairman's orders."

Raskob felt all the blood draining out of his face, but he held his ground. "You'll have to do better than that."

The head glowered at him for a long moment. "So you're going to be that way, soldier. What's your name?"

"Raskob. Private. I've got orders. What's the password?"

Ah, that comforting final redoubt—orders. That's the way life went in the FSE Armed Forces. You did nothing—not *thing one*—on your own initiative. But if you had orders you were . . . golden.

"Bear free spider."

"Castle, this is Sleeping Beauty. Confirm Prince Charming. I say again, confirm Prince Charming." *Asshole*.

"Send them in."

CHAPTER
SIXTEEN ─────────────

"Awesome performance, McKay," Sam Sloan said as his team leader slithered back down the hatch and slammed the lid. "Perfect impression of a real hardass. You'll get an Oscar."

"Up yours, too."

The car jolted into motion as the two troopies swung open the gate before them. It rolled forward a few meters through the wire and stopped to await the coming of a jeep to guide them to their appointment with the base CO. "This is never going to work," McKay said sourly.

"Sure it will, Billy," Casey said. "Piece of cake."

Sitting on the edge of a fold-down seat, tapping his fingertips on his knees, MacGregor grinned. "Sure it will work, Lieutenant." He looked ten years younger beneath the crew cut Tom Rogers had given him. Even McKay was startled by the transformation; he'd spent a lot of time with the man, and without his customary longish hair he might have passed him on the street without recognizing him.

"They're never going to be dumb enough to fall for this."

"Think about it. Assume for a moment I wasn't the President of the United States. On the other hand, if I were presented to, say, Sergeant William McKay with the U.S. peacekeeping force in Beirut, 1982, *and* I had the appropriate authentication to back me up—would you, as Sergeant Mc-Kay, doubt for a moment I was who I said I was?''

"Hell no! Grunts don't even rate wondering about shit like that. And I was just a corporal in the Root—sir.''

"Let me tell you, a staff-ranked Navy man wouldn't have behaved any differently," Sam Sloan said, grinning.

"Paper reality is where it's at, man," Casey said from the driver's seat.

"Or data-reality.'' Whoever this vehicle was intended for originally, they had the clearance for *everything*—including direct access to Chairman Maximov himself. Their communication several hours before with the contact Jake Morgenstern had given them inside Kirtland had been brief and to the point. And afterwards they had decided on this—the ballsiest approach possible, next to simply rolling in with all guns blazing to John Wayne it out with the sixty-odd men of the Effsee garrison, but also the one everybody reckoned most likely to succeed. Even McKay, even though he was griping about it now.

A pair of headlights came dipping and booming across the runway at them. "Looks like our guide," McKay said. "Let's ride.''

"I still don't like it," FSE expeditionary force Captain Robert Pickett said. He was a man of medium height and no excess weight, his brown hair swept back and thinning, his face composed of smoothed-off angles. He wore plain OD fatigues. He was sitting in an auditorium chair behind the desk of his little office looking worried in the auburn glow of a kerosene lamp.

"Nonsense," Political Officer Norwood said. The PO was shorter than Pickett, with a shock of tow-colored hair and a face that looked like it had been taken out of a tree trunk with two swipes of a sharp ax. "Our visitors are here on a high-priority mission. That's all there is to it.''

"It sure doesn't have to do with anything I know about.''

Norwood sniffed. "Operatives who deal at that clearance level don't usually report on their doings to captains.''

Pickett felt his gut twist with dislike of the man. But there was nothing he could do. According to the Federated States of Europe's Armed Forces regs a political officer automatically held rank on a par with that of the highest-ranking military officer on the scene. Even though he was a lousy civilian; even if he was the equivilant of a lousy GS-9 clerk-typist in his own organization. Norwood was a commissar, and that was all there was to it. Another FSE adaptation of Soviet military doctrine, along with the absolute pyramid-of-command principle—and maybe old General Mark Shaw shouldn't have tossed in the towel at Maximov's feet quite so easily.

Captain Pickett had been leading a squadron of Seventh Cavalry Bradleys against the Soviets when the balloon went up, and his team had been winning. With both sides cut off from their homelands, no hope of resupply or reinforcement, he could have taken the Russians; he knew it in his bones. But Mark Shaw had said uncle and that went for all American soldiers in the European theater. Even Captain Pickett, whose recommendation for a Medal of Honor was never going to be acted on.

"I still say we should at least check back with a higher authority," he said.

Norwood whipped him a white-eyed look that instantly slipped into a sneer. "And who would you take it up with? The Chairman?"

"How about General Price?"

"There's some possibility our communications have been compromised. These Americans—" He said the words, *these Americans*, as if they tasted like shit on his tongue. As if he weren't an American himself. *You rotten little turncoat. I'd like to break your lousy—* "These Americans are devilishly ingenious with the technological toys on which they lavish so much time and energy. Even after that same technology has destroyed the world, even when they have to scrape and struggle for survival—still they cling to their damn gadgets."

"If they busted open our communications," Pickett said evenly, "maybe they're not just gadgets."

Norwood wagged his head like a wet terrier. "I simply cannot talk to you, Captain. I realize for such an insignificant command even the military wouldn't waste a man of talent, but under the circumstances I think it unfortunate. We may be faced here with a situation crucial to this country's future."

And we might be faced with an invasion from Mars. The midnight message that came in flagged with the drop-everything top-drawer priority code had been anything but specific —except to state that some danger was imminent, and that every effort should be bent toward helping the special team they were waiting for to deal with it.

A knock at the door. It opened a crack to reveal the face of Lieutenant Abeyta. "Major Wayne and Captain Godfrey are here, sir. They've got Mr. Shirley with them."

Pickett looked to Norwood. "Send them in."

The door opened all the way and a civilian walked in, followed by the two most obvious cowboys Captain Pickett had seen in his entire life. Not "cowboy" of the local range-riding, bronc-busting type. But that unique blend of soldier of fortune and perpetual adolescent, that dweller in the military demimonde, that went by the same name. Instantly the skin all along the captain's back began to crawl.

He looked at the one on the left first. It was hard not to; that sucker was *big*. Six feet three if he was an inch, with short dirty-blond hair chopped off into tight greasy-looking ringlets. He was wearing some kind of outlandish gray and black and brown and white camouflage smock, and over that a shoulder holster carrying some sort of gigantic double-action revolver with outsized grips. To top it all off he had on what appeared to be a pair of yellow shooting glasses, for God's sake. His buddy was a little calmer: tall but not so tall, blade lean rather than massive, just a little too handsome, smoking a pipe and wearing dark glasses. In all Captain Pickett's experience, only motorcycle cops and special-ops soldiers wore sunglasses at night. He didn't think highly of either.

And the civilian. Black jacket, black tie, white shirt, black pants as shiny as his patent leather shoes. His long narrow face was on the handsome side, but all in all if you'd stuck dark glasses on him, he would have looked just like a Blues Brother. *CIA*, the captain thought. *Another one of Maximov's turncoats.* Pickett repressed a smile, knowing that Norwood would mark it down as a sign of inappropriate frivolity. *If only he* really *knew what I was thinking.*

He stood, slowly, to the edge of insolence. "And what may

I do for you . . . gentlemen? I'm Captain Pickett," he added, almost as an afterthought.

The civilian stepped forward and shook his hand. The grip was just the slightest touch, and put Pickett in mind of a dead carp. "I'm Shirley. This is Major Wayne"—a nod left to the handsome one—"and Captain Godfrey." A nod at the linebacker.

"A pleasure. Please sit down."

Shirley sat. His pet baboons stayed standing. Without asking permission Wayne took a pipe from the breast pocket of his cammie blouse, tamped it down, and lit up. Pickett hid his smile again. Norwood hated smoking, and a quick sidewise glance confirmed that his face had the consistency of paper that had been wet down and allowed to dry. "Yes?"

"Actually, Captain, I need to talk to your men as well as yourself. Your *loyal* men."

Irritation that the interloper hadn't told him he'd wanted a meeting with the troops turned to irritation at the implied aspersion. "Just exactly what do you mean, Mr. Shirley? My men are all loyal."

"Come now, Captain. How can you be so positive?"

"The captain is from the firing-line end of things, Mr. Shirley," Norwood said, smirking. "I fear he's rather divorced from the political realities."

A smile touched Shirley's mouth but not his eyes. "You take my meaning, I see. Why did you think I asked you to be sure FSE troops met us at the gate? You've got trouble here, Captain; bad trouble."

Oh shit, Pickett thought. In the three months he had been at Kirtland, he'd done everything he could to establish rapport with the local troops. They had fought so hard to survive, to maintain some semblance of pride in outfit, in a country they wanted to believe battered but undefeated. And it seemed that Political Officer Norwood had fought him every inch of the way. And now—*I can smell a witch-hunt.*

"I want all your expeditionary force personnel assembled in the most convenient structure at"—a glance at his wristwatch—"oh-three-hundred hours."

Pickett blinked in amazement. "But it's past two-thirty now!"

"Then you are going to have to snap it up, aren't you, Captain!"

Hangars being what they are—mostly empty space—they react curiously to the dynamic overpressure of a thermonuclear explosion. They either get blown clean away or they continue to just stand there as if nothing had happened. A couple of the ones near the apron on Kirtland had continued just to stand. This one was being used as a storage area, bales of stores and spare parts stacked next to plastic bags of precious high-octane aviation fuel. The other major surviving hangar, in use as a shop, had soldiers working in it who'd been here when the expeditionary force arrived; no way to clear them out without awakening suspicions. Though how this nitwit Shirley thought his midnight confab was going to avoid attracting the attention of the other hundred and fifty people on base was totally beyond him. Oh well; he was an Effsee now, too, and he had his orders. Nobody said they had to make sense.

Standing at his side, Shirley nodded in apparent satisfaction, his face pale but pleased in the light of battery-powered work lamps hanging from overhead. "Good job, good job. Is this everyone, Captain?"

"We've got a few people on duty we couldn't pull off without arousing suspicion. And I didn't think *all* the military police on duty should be members of the local garrison. Do you?"

Shirley's eyebrows rose. "You mean you permit people other than expeditionary force personnel to perform police duties?"

Pickett felt his neck getting very warm inside his collar. "Now, just wait a minute here." He sensed Norwood sidling near, ears pulled up into little points. He was past caring. "I don't know what you believe is going on here. But all the personnel on this base are loyal, obedient soldiers. They—Jesus! Hold on there, Major Wayne, sir!"

The sunglassed major paused with his lighter hovering over the bowl of his pipe. "I wouldn't do that if I were you, sir," Pickett said. He nodded toward the orange bladders heaped against one wall. "Fuel. One spark lands wrong and *whoosh!*"

Looking sheepish, Wayne put his paraphernalia away. Godfrey stiffened. He cocked his head, seemed to listen. Then he came forward and bent down to whisper in Shirley's ear.

"Excuse me, Captain, Political Officer Norwood. There's a communication coming through for me in the vehicle," Shirley said. He walked out the little access door inset in the big sliding door with the hulking Godfrey in tow.

Major Wayne made small talk with Norwood, pitched just low enough that Pickett could hear it without being able to derive the sense of it. He ignored them, staring off at all directions, looking at the surly, sleepy men standing around rubbing their eyes or sitting on carts and crates griping about having been hauled out of the sack in the middle of the night.

Fifteen whole minutes later, in came Shirley and his big ugly shadow again. Shirley nodded to Norwood and Pickett and then clambered up on the hood of a little Subaru service vehicle. "Gentlemen, I thank you for your patience. But I'm afraid I've brought you here under false pretenses. I hope you'll understand. You see, this structure has now been surrounded by forces of the United States of America, and I'm calling upon you as soldiers of the Federated States of Europe expeditionary force to lay down your arms. You will be treated as prisoners of war; no one will be harmed."

Wayne and Godfrey were suddenly standing shoulder to shoulder in front of Shirley, guns drawn. "Everybody fall in!" Godfrey bellowed. "The line forms on the right."

"Jesus Christ!" One of the mouths quit gaping long enough to holler, "That's Jeff MacGregor!"

"Fucking-A straight," snarled Captain Godfrey.

"And we are the Guardians!"

With mongoose speed, Political Officer Norwood whipped a small hand weapon from the pocket of his pants and fired. Hissing, a line of magenta fire streaked forward and struck smack in the center of Billy McKay's huge chest, knocking him back onto the hood of the Subaru.

CHAPTER
SEVENTEEN ─────────

Jeff MacGregor jumped down into cover on the far side of the vehicle. Sam Sloan swung McKay's borrowed .45 to blow the little commissar away, but the white-blond man had ducked behind Captain Pickett. Then the startled Effsees were exploding in all directions. Several lunged forward, grabbing up hand tools as makeshift clubs, and Sloan sprang into the seat of the open car to protect the President.

Sitting on his ass on the cement floor of the hangar, Billy McKay looked down at his chest. A miniature red sun seemed to be burning in the center of it. It was a flare, fired from a small repeating pistol. Just the sort of sneaky, hateful weapon a scumbag like Norwood could be expected to carry. If it hadn't been for the Kevlar vest McKay wore under his urban-warfare camo blouse, the evil little projectile would be inside his ribcage now, cooking out his lights and liver. As it was, it was melting the Kevlar, and was not too fucking comfortable. With his left hand McKay jerked Casey Wilson's Gerber combat knife from its sheath, dug the point of the narrow leaf-shaped blade under the projectile, and flipped it spitting across the floor.

Somebody lunged at him. He slammed the eight-and-three-quarter inch barrel of Casey's Dirty Harry .44 across the bridge of the man's nose. Squalling, the man went down. McKay heard a shot, spun around to see men falling back from the Subaru where Sloan was trying to maintain a Weaver combat stance with his feet in the front seat, leaving a man writhing on the cement in the midst of a spreading crimson stain. McKay poked the Smith and Wesson into the air and blasted off two more shots. Their thunder brought conversation to a halt.

"That's enough, you assholes! This goddamned place really is surrounded and if you fuck with me anymore, I'm gonna really start kicking asses and taking names—"

"You'll fry first!"

McKay cut off, turned his head. That was the sort of comment that caught your attention right off. That little white-haired weasel Norwood was backing toward the door aiming his flare pistol at the fuel bladders. "Just one squeeze of the trigger, and we all burn. Including your precious President, Guardian McKay. Throw down your weapons and give up, then tell the fools outside to surrender. Or we all burn. Life to the Chairman! Long live the Federated States of Europe!"

"Hit it, Case," McKay said under his breath. Norwood glared at him with wildfire eyes. "What's that? Speak up."

"You lose," McKay said.

The squeal of tires on cement sounded from the night behind Norwood. The commissar started to turn his head, and then ten tons of Cadillac Gage Super Commando came smashing through the sliding door of the hangar and squashed him like a bug.

"I can't tell you gentlemen how grateful we are," Lieutenant Alex Garcia said, sitting over coffee with the President and the Guardians in a kerosene-lit cinderblock commissary. "It's been hell, these last few months."

"How are you planning to dispose of the prisoners?" Sloan asked. Just as Jeff MacGregor had announced to the assembled expeditionary force personnel, the hangar had been surrounded by a score of non-FSE personnel armed with weapons liberated from the storeroom established as an armory with some quick quiet help from Tom Rogers. It was to complete these arrangements that Billy McKay had momentarily escorted MacGregor out of the hangar just before the briefing. And it had only been over McKay's strenuous objections that MacGregor had gone back in, but MacGregor insisted on playing his role out. It had almost gotten him killed. Scratching at the bandage on his chest under his camouflaged blouse, McKay winced. What the fuck; grunts were *supposed* to get knocked around.

Garcia's face wrapped itself in a look of concern. Like the rest of him, it was a bit on the round side, dark, with a trim dark mustache. "I'm not really sure, give most of them a chance to switch sides if they want. If they don't—" A shrug.

MacGregor frowned. "What then?"

"I suppose disarm them, load 'em into a spare vehicle and let them go. The rest, the ones who are just too hard-core, those I guess we lock up."

MacGregor relaxed. He'd obviously been afraid a harsher fate awaited the FSE prisoners; post-holocaust justice tended to be summary and swift.

"Besides, you got the worst one," said Richter, the big, dark-haired Air Force sergeant at his side. "That Norwood—he was a real bear."

"What's going to become of Captain Pickett?" MacGregor asked.

Garcia hesitated, obviously a little taken aback to be talking to the President of the United States in person. "Well, I, I don't know, Mr. President. I hope he decides to come in with us."

"Bet he won't," Richter commented.

Garcia nodded. "The Captain is a great man, just great. He always looked out for the men—all the men, not just the Effsees. He's a good leader, firm and fair. And he always tried to shelter those of us who weren't Effsees from that sonofabitch Norwood—sorry, Mr. President."

MacGregor smiled and inclined his head. "I don't see any reason to take exception to your evaluation, son."

"If Pickett hadn't been FSE, we might really have warmed to him. But as for joining us—" A shrug. "He may, he may not. He disapproved of a lot of stuff he had to do as an expeditionary force officer—a lot more toward the end. You could tell. But he's got this funny sense of honor. If he feels bound to the FSE, he'll stick with them till the bitter end."

"What's going to become of you?" Sam Sloan asked.

Another shrug. "Who knows? We might try to hold here."

"Unless the Effsees want the joint back," Richter said. "And they might. They don't have much transcontinental air traffic yet, but what they have, comes through here."

Garcia sighed. "Or we could just split. The survivors in Albuquerque don't like us much anymore, not since the FSE came to town. But we could still do a quick fade. Go up in the mountains, maybe. Or head north or south."

Garcia sipped his coffee and shook his head. "It's been pretty heavy, pretty strange. When the expeditionary force got here, we thought, 'Hey! that's cool. Somebody's finally putting it all together.' And Wild Bill Lowell back. I mean, I didn't vote for the man, but you guys are military, *you* know. You feel comfortable with him." He shook his head. "But shit, he turned out like the Ayatollah or something. Just another crazy dictator."

Sam Sloan smiled a secret smile. McKay just sat and looked stonefaced. "I've been wondering something, Lieutenant," Casey Wilson said. "Like, how did you happen to be in touch with Dr. Morgenstern out in California?"

"Well, I guess you know about our secret transmitter." There were nods all around; that was how the Guardians had gotten in touch with the loyal troops on Kirtland Base, late last night. "Well, we've been passing coded messages back and forth since, hell, not long after the War. Started while you guys were out in California, as a matter of fact. Lately we've been slipping them in among the Effsees' traffic, nobody noticed worth a damn."

Sloan looked incredulous. "But why?"

"Well, for one thing, a couple of our pilots trained with the Israeli Air Force, back in the late seventies when Dr. Morgenstern was with the Israeli Ministry of Defense for a while. They got to know him then. But there was somebody else he knew in the area, too."

He turned around, nodded towards a plumpish man in green fatigues, who had been hanging shyly back beside the coffee machine. The man bobbed his head, smiled, came shyly

forward. In the canteen gloom, McKay had taken him for
another Hispanic, but as he came closer he saw the man was
Eastern Indian.

"This is Dr. Churi Srinarampa. He's a biochemist. He was
up in Santa Fe. Wandered down in the late winter—unfortunately, just about the time the Effsees turned up."

The Guardians turned their heads expectantly toward the
Indian, wondering what the hell this was about. He bobbed his
head and grinned an exceedingly white grin. "I am very much
pleased to meet you gentlemen," he said in a high-pitched,
nasal voice. "You have come for the blueprints, yes?"

The Guardians stared at him in stunned amazement. "You've
got to be kidding," Sam Sloan said.

Srinarampa blinked rapidly. His eyes were large and moist.
"I do not understand. Do you not come for the blueprints?"

"Jesus Christ on a skateboard," McKay said in disgust.
MacGregor was looking totally confused. "We come looking
for a hidey-hole out here in the desert, and we run smack into
another goddamn Blueprint participant."

His vehemence pushed the doctor back a step. "Never mind
him, Doctor," Sam said hurriedly. "We're just, ah, somewhat
surprised to find you here."

"So what are we going to do with him?" McKay asked.

"Take him with us, of course," Sloan said.

"Risky," Tom Rogers said.

"And we're, like, not totally sure of the sort of reception
we'll get at our . . . destination," Casey observed.

The Indian doctor's smile was becoming very brittle. "Why,
of course, we'll take him along," MacGregor said. McKay's
reference to the Blueprint had finally clued him in. "Once I'm
relocated, reassembling the Blueprint will become a number-
one priority again."

McKay looked around, uncomfortable about discussing
top-secret affairs in front of just anybody. "Whatever." He
stood up, sretched, yawned. "If you dudes can dig up a bunk
for me, I'm going to log some rack time."

The lieutenant's eyebrows rose. "But the sun's coming up,"
he protested. "We have something to show you."

"Can't it wait?" McKay asked grumpily.

More diplomatic, Sloan said, "We've been a long time without sleep. And it's been an eventful night."

Garcia and Richter both stood up. "But we wanted you to see," the lieutenant said. "We just didn't expect you to charge in and rescue us out of the goodness of your hearts. We have every intention of paying you back."

"That's very commendable, and we're grateful," Sam Sloan said. "But—"

"So come on out and see your surprise," Richter said.

"Oh, wow," Casey Wilson said.

"A C-130S Super Hercules," Richter said proudly. "The pride of Albuquerque."

The cargo plane loomed huge and black in the first pale sprinkling of sunlight from the cliffs to the east. At first glance it looked just like any other Herkie to McKay. And then Casey and crew chief Richter got involved in an enthusiastic discussion in which McKay could only understand every third word, and that only because every sixth one Casey said, "Oh, wow," again.

As a fighter pilot born and bred, Casey might have been expected to feel only lordly contempt for a dumpy, slow transport. And of course not even he would classify a Hercules, no matter how special, with purebred fighters like his beloved F-16. But Casey was also a genuine flying nut, and this Hercules was not only a classic of aviation but a modern marvel as well. Forty years after the design had first flown, the stubby four-engined propeller-driven transport was still the workhorse aircraft for most of the world. The explosion in aviation design of the 1980s had produced a lot of new knowledge that pointed the way to radical changes in aerodynamic design. In the meantime, it was being applied to existing airframes such as the C-130 to extend the design's life far beyond what the original designers could ever have conceived.

What they were looking at was new production, mottled green and brown and tan above, painted black on the underside and sides clear up to the level of the high-mounted wings. McKay was instantly lost by the talk about graphite-epoxy frame and winglets and whatnot. But he could see that the big wing had a lot of what looked like little fins mounted on it that he didn't remember seeing on any of the hundreds of normal Herkies that he had ridden in the past. And then there were the props. Not four straight blades, but nine of the goddamn things, short and broad and curving backwards like scimitar blades.

"With the new-design props and the winglets, we don't just get radical improvement in maneuverability. This baby is built for speed and endurance. We are talking eight hundred klicks an hour, and we're talking about doing it at thirty thousand feet for five thousand kilometers with fifty metric tons of cargo."

"Far out," Casey said.

"Yeah, well, I'm sure this is just the greatest thing since sliced bread," McKay said. He found himself hugging himself slightly against the dawn chill. Here it was the beginning of July, and how could it be so damned cold in the desert, for Chrissake? "But I don't see what that has to do with us."

They were circling the big airplane, smelling aviation fuel and sagey desert vegetation while technicians in orange coveralls scampered around with hoses and clipboards and did busy flightline-preparation things. Dr. Churi Srinarampa trotted dutifully along behind, grinning with a certain terrible determination. Lt. Garcia stopped short. "Don't you understand, Lieutenant McKay? Wherever you're going, within the continental United States—and you don't have to tell us in advance —this baby'll take you. A lot more quickly—not to mention comfortably—than you could make it in your armored car."

"Well I'll be dipped in shit," Sam Sloan said, "and fried for a hush puppy."

"I certainly hope not," MacGregor said. "You mean you're offering us the use of this aircraft, Lieutenant? That's awfully generous of you."

"Not at all, sir. You're the President, our Commander in Chief. It's no more than our duty. And I'll tell you, sir: unless you are flying to Alaska, that baby will take you where you want to go and then come home without having to stop at a gas station."

"Great," McKay said, still fuzzy and not quite grasping

the import of what was going on. "But what will we do with Mobile One?"

"Billy, the Super Herkie has a capacity of fifty tons," Casey said. "Mobile One weighs ten."

"Oh." A Super Commando in a Super Hercules. McKay thought it was silly that every time a manufacturer decided to upgrade an existing design they tacked "Super" onto its name. Like the way Cadillac Gage had done when they revamped their old V-150 Commando. He guessed it was too late to complain now. "So when will she be ready to go?" he asked, already dreading the answer.

Richter's square face split in a grin. "Hell, right now, if you say so!"

McKay looked to the others. He shrugged his shoulders expressively, as if to ask, *well?*

"Let's do it, Billy," Tom Rogers said. "We ain't getting any younger."

"Mr. President?"

MacGregor was grinning almost as enormously as Richter. "Not to disparage our noble vehicle, but those fold-down seats are getting awfully tedious on my tailbone. And just think! I haven't actually *flown* in over a year. We can travel to our safe haven in style!"

"You really can load Mobile One onto this beast?" McKay asked.

"That's affirmative," Richter said. "We can start—"

A young airman with a little mustache that made him look like a chipmunk came trotting up and tugged at Garcia's sleeve. "Sorry to bother you, sir. But there's a high-priority communication coming in from expeditionary force command in California."

Garcia showed the Guardians a wink. "This might be worth listening to. What channel's it on?"

"All of them, sir. Military and civilian. It's announcing a press conference for oh-seven-hundred and everyone in America—military and civilian—is ordered to tune in."

"My fellow Americans," the baritone voice of General Alan Price said from the receiver in Pickett's old office. "I come before you to bring you news of the greatest importance for this nation and its ally, the Federated States of Europe.''

'Wow,'' Casey said. "He sounds just like Lyndon Johnson.''

"You're too young to remember LBJ,'' Sam said.

"I saw old film strips on television.''

"Will everyone kindly shut the hell up and let the man speak?'' McKay demanded.

"As you know, former Vice President Jeffrey MacGregor was tried in the spring for treason for attempting to usurp the rightful authority of President William Lowell. He was sentenced to death. The execution was to be carried out at dawn tomorrow.

"Now I must tell you he has added a crime more heinous still, if that's even possible: the murder of the President of the United States of America.''

CHAPTER
EIGHTEEN ─────────────

Billy McKay felt as if the eyes of the world were fixed on him personally.

"Less than two weeks ago, a team of saboteurs and terrorists infiltrated a maximum-security installation called Heartland, in the former state of Iowa. That facility had, for slightly over a year, been the seat of government for the United States of America. The saboteurs, led by a team of turncoats called the Guardians—acting in a perversion of their original mission, which was to protect the life of the President of the United States—liberated the traitor Jeffrey MacGregor and destroyed the complex. This wanton act of destruction led to the deaths of thousands of innocent civilian technicians and loyal soldiers of the Federated States of Europe's expeditionary force.

"It also resulted, I very much regret to announce, in the death of the President of the United States, William Lowell."

There was more. It got lost in the roaring in McKay's ears. The bastards had gone public. And they were accusing the Guardians and Jeff MacGregor of the most terrible crime in the nation's history.

Garcia and Richter were staring at them with hard eyes. Srinarampa looked from one to the other, not quite understanding what all this was about.

"What the hell," Richter said at last, "is going on here?"

"Is all this true?" Garcia sputtered.

"Of course it ain't," Richter said. "It's just the usual Eff-see bullshit. But I'd still like to know how much of it, if any, is straight." He looked very hard at Jeff MacGregor.

Everybody looked at MacGregor. They were skating on very thin ice, McKay realized. Within a few heartbeats of being seized and imprisoned—possibly shot out of hand—by the very men they'd just liberated. No amount of friendship or good feeling would be sufficient to overlook treason.

"It's true," MacGregor said. "Some of it. But General Price is not telling the whole story. It goes like this."

And he told it all. Starting with the creation of Project Blueprint and its parallel, Project Guardian, years ago under the direction of the shadowy Major Crenna. About how the Guardians were originally assembled and trained under the pretext that their sole mission was to escort the President to safe haven—even as they were doing now—in the event of nuclear war. How in the face of all prior planning Bill Lowell had decided to trust his life to his National Emergency Airborne Command Post and leave his elite Guardians on the ground, watching over Vice President MacGregor in the White House. How Lowell's plane was lost during the attack, with no contact to indicate where it went down or what had become of it. How he—Jeff MacGregor—was sworn in as President, and began his run through the fires of a shattered America to the shelter of Heartland.

He told of how the Guardians learned of their true mission —the reassembly of the Blueprint for Renewal—from Major Crenna himself while they were in Heartland. Of their spending the intervening year searching for the pieces of the Blueprint, the master key to which had been lost with Lowell. Of their battles with road gypsies and Josiah Coffin's inspired hordes, their defeat of Lieutenant Governor van Damm's revolutionaries, bit by bit piecing the Blueprint back together.

And then: invasion. Heartland seized in a lightning attack by FSE troops—all its sophisticated defenses obligingly open-

ing to the invaders because they had with them the man with
the keys, Wild Bill Lowell himself. MacGregor imprisoned
and tortured, the Guardians treacherously led into ambush by
expeditionary force troops. Their escape, only to be captured
by Sergeant Marla Eklund and India Three, and how only
Heartland's incredible blunder of sending Soviet paratroops
serving with the expeditionary force had prevented Eklund
from dutifully turning her captives over to the FSE.

He recounted how William Lowell had been only the insane
shell of his former self, a demented marionette whose strings
were worked by the mysterious Trajan. Trajan—otherwise
known as W. Soames Summerill, conservative gadfly and
bestselling novelist, secretly head of a faction within the Central Intelligence Agency that, in the wake of the One-Day War,
had seized control of the Company at the behest of Chairman
Maximov. He told of Maximov's plan to use Trajan and a willing Bill Lowell to loot the United States of her most precious
resources, including, especially, the Blueprint for Renewal.

His voice shaking with emotion, MacGregor told of being
tried *in absentia* for treason, sentenced to die on the Fourth of
July. He told of the hardships the Guardians had undergone
as they fought their way toward Heartland in the final confrontation with America's twisted overlords. Of how they and
their allies had penetrated Heartland and escaped with Jeff
MacGregor and the rescued Blueprint personnel—but only at
the cost of Heartland's destruction and the death of Major
Crenna. How they'd been running ever since Dexter White's
treason, the failures in Denver and California.

Which brought them here, with their lives in the hands of
the Kirtland garrison.

"But you did it?" Richter asked. "You killed Bill Lowell?"

MacGregor's eyes flicked momentarily in McKay's direction. "Yes. President Lowell lost his life in the attack on
Heartland."

Richter's big fist boomed down on the desk, threatening to
upset the kerosene lamp. "Good! The sonofabitch sold his
country down the river. He was playing into the hands of the
likes of that cocksucker Norwood, and he knew it."

Garcia was nodding, smiling grimly. The Indian doctor was
nodding and smiling too. His English was obviously none too

hot. McKay hoped he was a hell of a biochemist. "May I tell our people this, Mr. President? What you've just told me?"

MacGregor turned to McKay, who grimaced, and rubbed his massive chin. This was a national security matter of the highest import, and the President was looking right at him. "What the fuck?" he said. "Do it."

"I think we owe your people the truth," MacGregor said.

Garcia nodded to Richter. "Let's go have a talk with the boys." They stood. The lieutenant looked at MacGregor. "I hope you gentlemen understand, but I must ask you to stay here."

"Under guard?" Rogers said.

"Negative. But please don't leave this office, all the same." The two went out.

"Do you think we sold him, or was he just trying to lull us?" Sam Sloan asked.

"I think he understands," MacGregor said. "For our sakes —for the sake of this country—I hope he does."

"I guess we'll soon find out." McKay stretched his long legs out before him, folded his arms across his chest, put his chin on his collarbone, and went to sleep.

He was dreaming confusedly of dangling in that huge ventilation shaft that led down into the guts of Heartland, with Marla Eklund's voice screaming for help from somewhere below, when a touch on the arm jerked him to consciousness. "What?" he barked, his reclaimed .45 halfway out of its holster.

It was Tom Rogers, standing, with an old campaigner's reflexes, well away from McKay and to the side. "Garcia is coming." McKay blinked the sleep from his eyes and got up.

Garcia came in alone. "I told the men what you told me, Mr. President."

"And?"

He ducked his head back out the door. "Come on in." McKay's hand closed around the black rubber Pachmayr grips of his .45. Was he calling the security boys to haul them off?

Instead four men wearing flight suits walked in. "These are Lieutenant Reed, Chief Warrant Officer Olivarez, Sergeant Blum, and Sergeant Wu. They'll be your flight crew."

• • •

Bill McKay had ridden in a Hercules so often he felt like leaving a damage deposit. He was used to a long, slow roll down the runway, with a gentle liftoff at the end, even though he knew the beast could perform a lot more briskly when it needed to. He'd even experienced some of the Herkie's short takeoff and landing parameters on stop-and-go training with Force RECON and the Studies and Observations Group, Southwest Asia Command. And none of it had prepared him for this.

The rest of his team, including MacGregor and the Indian biochemist, were lashed into the seats bolted in the forward part of the cargo compartment, up ahead of where Mobile One sat chained to the deck plating and wrapped with some kind of superstrong plastic strapping that looked to McKay like saltwater taffy and was supposed to ensure that the big car went nowhere. Not McKay. As commander of this traveling sideshow he got the privilege of sitting out the takeoff in the navigator's seat, aft of copilot Olivarez. Wu, the compact handsome navigator with a trim, black mustache, was strapped into the crew bunk up at the top of the bulkhead behind.

Reed grinned back at him. He was blond, a definite "Robert Redford in his younger days" type, only taller. "Ready, Lieutenant."

"Go for it."

"Everybody strapped in?" Olivarez said over the intercom.

The passengers all answered in the affirmative. The engines were growling low steady white noise. Suddenly they began to roar, and the seat hit Billy McKay in the back. And while he was still trying to adjust himself to the huge plane charging off like a dragster, that baby pitched her nose up and slid off into the sky.

"Far *out!*" Casey gasped.

"Can they *do* that?" McKay demanded.

"That's progress, Lieutenant McKay," Blum said from the systems engineer's seat to Billy's left. He was the thin intense type, with a long straight nose and a shock of brown hair.

"We'll be leveling off at our cruising altitude in about fifteen minutes," Reed said. "We'll let you know in case you other gentlemen want to come up and take a look around."

McKay was still swallowing hard at the abruptness of take-off when they were passing over the mountains—round masses cut off in sharp edges on their western face rather than pointy peaks, clustered thick with tall pine forests on the heights and dotted with scrub, dried green on brown in the lower slopes and valleys. "Pretty country," Olivarez said. From the proprietary tone in his voice it sounded as if he were from this part of the world. "Prettier up north, though."

McKay grunted. From the mountains west, the terrain reminded him altogether too much of the Midwest, where he'd spent so much of his life and almost lost it. And east—"That's the Great Plains starting up down there, ain't it?" He nodded his chin at the land smoothing out to dun flatness below.

"That's affirmative," Reed said.

"That means the scenery don't change from here to the Mississippi Valley."

Reed looked at his copilot and shrugged. "Well, that's not exactly accurate—"

McKay nodded brusquely. "Right. You boys have yourselves a fine time up here; I'm going back and going to sleep."

The Hercules crew looked at one another. "Aren't you forgetting something, Lieutenant?" Wu asked.

"What's that?"

"Bill could maybe use some idea of where to steer for," Reed said, "seeing as you're letting him have his seat back."

McKay paused, standing there braced as the plane leveled out over the plains of eastern New Mexico. It was actually hard for him to say their destination. Almost as if the Effsees would be listening in on their cockpit conversation. It was silly, he knew—and, anyway, that slick son of a bitch Vesensky or Victor or whatever the fuck his name was was probably two steps ahead of them already.

"Washington, D.C.," he said at last.

Reed pursed his lips and let loose a long low whistle. It seemed to sum up the general sentiment. "Wake me when we hit KC," McKay said.

"Why's that?" Wu asked.

"So I can take a dump over Dexter White's head."

A few minutes after McKay left, Casey Wilson pushed forward through the crew entryway low on the port of the plane and climbed up the ladder to the flight deck. "Lieutenant Wilson," Reed greeted him. "A pleasure to see you."

The others echoed him. There was a certain awe in their voices. Casey Wilson was definitely the *numero uno* aerial hero of recent times. As a courtesy, acknowledgement of his status, Kirtland had given him a spare G-suit to wear.

"Come up to watch the scenery?" Olivarez asked. "Your *compadre* thought it was so dull it put him to sleep."

Casey glanced out the big semicircle of windows, which stretched across the blunt nose of the aircraft. "It is pretty dull," he admitted. He looked around, a poignant look on his boyish face. "I just wondered if you guys would mind if I came up here and, like, talked shop awhile."

Somewhere over Texas Sam Sloan wandered up, yawning and stretching, rubbing sleep from his brown eyes. Casey was stacked in the copilot's seat, talking animatedly with hands and mouth in the time-approved fighter pilot manner. The four crewmen were gathered around, listening raptly and not paying any attention to their driving. Sloan guessed the plane was on autopilot. At least he hoped it was.

"Thought I'd come forward and make sure you boys were headed in the right direction."

"Omigod!" Reed said, spinning around in mock alarm. "We haven't been watching the road! Quick, Bill, find out where we are!"

The navigator peered out at the flat landscape beneath, stippled with shadows from little wads of clouds drifting in a layer between plane and planet. "Looks like eastern Manitoba to me."

"Holy shit. Looks like we'll have to make turnaround in Alaska. Know anybody up that way, Commander?"

"The Soviet 2301st Special Airlanding Brigade."

The flight crew looked at him. "Are you shitting us?" the engineer asked.

"No, man, there's a whole brigade of Russians in Alaska," Casey explained.

Olivarez shook himself. "Gives me the creeps, having Red soldiers on American soil."

"There are Soviet troops with the expeditionary force," Wu said.

"Turncoats. Just like the rest of them." The stocky Chicano looked at Sloan. "You boys planning to do anything about that? About Alaska?"

Sam shrugged. "Since they're about three thousand klicks from the mainland, there's not a lot we can do to them right offhand. Then again, there's not much they can do to *us*." He smiled. "On the other hand, once we get settled in, I wouldn't be surprised if Bill McKay heads up there and cleans them out his own self."

"That commander of yours, he's a pretty hard-core dude, isn't he?" the copilot asked.

"He is that."

Blum stood up and stretched with a quick whippet flex. "I think I'll fix myself a sandwich and coffee in the galley. Do you want some?" Casey shook his head, too wrapped up in the experience of being airborne again to worry himself about anything so mundane as eating. Sam nodded. "And maybe we can see if the President wants us to take something back to him."

"Sounds like a good idea," Sam said. "I like your arrangements up here. You've got a galley and everything. That's what I call civilized—almost like being on a ship." Casey laughed. Sloan started to turn away, but his eye was caught by the flat landscape unrolling underneath.

"What beautiful country," he enthused. "Great farming land."

From this altitude, anyway, a lot more of the Midwest looked cultivated to Sam's experienced eye than he'd expected. Maybe the country wasn't in quite such terrible shape as he imagined; maybe life did go on, after all. They crossed the Mississippi Valley, and the country began to rumple up into the Eastern Coastal Range. The mountains were blue-green and changeless. Sam felt a sense of awe, of reverence almost. *We had so much,* he thought. *And we came so close to throwing it all away.*

From the mountains east the sky below them was curdling

into undercast. Olivarez was flying the airplane, Casey was sitting in the pilot's seat, and Reed was racked out in the bunk. Sloan was leaning against the navigator's desk. He felt a formless unease, something he couldn't quite put a name to.

They banked gently left. "What we're going to do, we're going to swing north and circle down over Baltimore to make our approach to D.C. Got anyplace in particular you'd like to set down?" said Olivarez.

"Have to ask the President and McKay. Somewhere on the outskirts," Sloan answered.

"No problem. All we need is a big enough level space, with pavement."

"Shouldn't be any problem," Casey commented. "There were, like, a lot of defunct factories in the area. Parking lots should be pretty empty."

Olivarez nodded off to starboard. The dense green carpet covering the mountains was interrupted by a broad swath of gray. "Dead zone. Must have caught some fallout. Radiation's death on pine forests."

"So what are our friends on the ground doing?" Sloan asked. He hated to think about the death of forests.

"Looks like they're doing something," flight engineer Blum said. His voice sounded oddly strained. "Somebody just started watching us." Sam looked around. Bright flashes of orange were strobing across an Electronic Counter Measures screen, bathing the engineer's face in quick flashes of light.

"Yeah," Olivarez said. "I'm getting it too. Early warning radar."

Casey sat up. "That's what's been bothering me, man," he said, echoing Sloan's thoughts perfectly. "This has been, like, too easy. Every klick we've gained since the War, we've had to fight for. And here we're flying across two-thirds of the country in just a couple of hours."

"Jesus, Lieutenant Wilson, don't say things like that," Olivarez said.

Reed was sitting up on his bunk. "Would you mind checking the radio, seeing if you could pick up any traffic?"

"Who could be looking at us with radar?" Sam wanted to know.

"Who do you think, Commander?" Reed asked. "Probably the same people who owned this airplane until about oh-three-hundred this morning."

"I'd better get McKay," Sloan said.

"No need to bother him," Reed said. "It's probably nothing to get—"

" . . . *bearing 315 from Downtown, one hundred fifty kilometers,*" a voice crackled from the speaker.

"*Roger that, Big Man. Eagle copy.*"

Sam cocked his head. "What's that you've got there, Case?"

Casey's face had gone very pale beneath its California tan. "It sounds an awful like GCI, Sam. Ground Controlled Interception—almost as if somebody's vectoring a fighter onto us."

"Negative to that 'as if,' " Blum said. "Our ECM gear indicates somebody's looking at us with target-tracking radar—and the readout says it's an F-15."

CHAPTER
NINETEEN ———————————

"This is too damned easy." Bill McKay woke up with the words in his brain, and half wondered whether he'd said them aloud himself. He looked around. Tom was stretched across a couple of the seats, dead to the world. Off by the side of the compartment MacGregor was playing chess with the doctor, using a little plastic traveling set the doctor had brought with him. McKay didn't know much about chess, but from the looks of things—a whole lot more of Dr. Srinarampa's black pieces on the board than MacGregor's white ones—the President was getting his clock well cleaned. He looked up.

"What's that, Billy?" he asked.

"Nothing, sir." McKay stood, stretched. "Think I'll go up front and see if we're about there." MacGregor nodded and went back to his game. McKay started forward to the hatchway that led to the cabin.

He'd only taken a few steps when Casey's voice in his ear stopped him. "Billy. I think we've got a problem."

"I've got them on radar now, Lieutenant," Blum said. "That bastard is closing fast."

"*Auto Acc lock-on affirmative,*" a voice crackled out of the speakers.

"*You are cleared to fire, Eagle. I say again, you are cleared to fire.*"

With the speed of a striking rattler, Casey's hand darted out and slapped the switch that unlocked and enabled his set of controls. "Lieutenant Wilson, what are you doing?" Reed asked from his bunk.

"*Hold on everybody!*" Casey hollered, and then he cranked the big airplane over hard on its left wing.

Standing behind Olivarez, Sam felt the deck hit him hard on the soles of his feet, buckling his knees. He grabbed the back of the seat, clung on. The blood seemed to be draining to the soles of his feet.

And then a ghastly orange light filled the cockpit, and thunder smote him.

Billy McKay was coming through the hatchway when suddenly this giant hand was pressing him down to the deck. Then the cockpit blew up before his very eyes.

When the roaring in his ears had receded and the green wash of afterimage began to fade from in front of his eyes he said, "Holy shit. We're dead."

"Negative, Billy," Casey's voice said in his ear. "Sparrow missile. Didn't hit us. But they're proximity fused, and this one went off thirty, forty meters away."

"Are you all right? What about Sam?"

"I think my ankle's sprained," Sloan said. His voice wasn't even shaky. This was the sort of thing he understood. "Other than that I'm whole, I think."

"I'm fine, Billy," Casey said. "Took some shrapnel, but my vest stopped it." A pause. "Lieutenant Reed is hurt pretty bad, and Wu's hit too." The crushing gee force eased as the airplane dropped back closer to level flight. "Better go check on Tom and the President, Billy. We're in a little bit of trouble."

"Is there some firing port in this goddamned airplane I can shoot out of?" McKay demanded.

"Negative, Billy. You go get the others into Mobile One and

strap them down. The armor ought to keep fragments off them when we get hit again."

"Goddamn it, if I've got to go out, I want to go out fighting!"

"Negative, Billy. There's nothing you can do. I say again, Billy, go back and buckle in."

McKay bridled. It sounded dangerously as if his subordinate was giving him orders. Then he thought about it. He was the undisputed leader of the Guardians. But their setup was flexible; whenever one man's expertise applied to a situation, he held effective command. This was Casey Wilson's element, not Bill McKay's. "Roger, Case," he said. "And one thing."

"What's that?"

"Don't embarrass us."

"Have I ever?"

McKay raced for the rear of the plane, Sloan limping at his heels.

The cockpit looked like a penthouse of hell, with good outdoors exposure. The near-miss by the missile had torn jagged chunks in the roof of the cabin, letting in a fierce whistling cold wind that cut right through to the bones, and glints of sky so blue it hurt the eye.

"Lieutenant Reed is dead," Wu said.

The flight engineer was checking Wu's wounds. "You're not in such good shape yourself, Bill." The navigator shrugged him off.

"You two get strapped in," Olivarez said. "Shit. Poor Keith."

"Do I have your permission to keep control of this aircraft, Chief?" Casey asked.

Olivarez paused. "That's affirmative, sir." A quick grin. "She's in the best possible hands."

But he couldn't keep from his face the conviction that not even the consummate skill of Casey Wilson could save them. Behind him, his two fellow crew members exchanged glances as they strapped themselves down. Lieutenant Wilson was a living legend, yes. But it was years, to the best of their knowledge, since he had flown an airplane in combat, a year at least since he'd flown at all. And flying an aircraft in combat is the

same as any athletic endeavor: it requires constant practice
to keep the muscles in requisite trim, the senses and reflexes
tuned to perfection. *Did Casey still have it?*

If he didn't they were dead.

On the other hand, if he did nothing . . . they were dead
anyway.

"We're strapped into the car," McKay's voice said in
Wilson's ear. "Jeff hurt his arm, but I don't think it's broken.
Why the hell ain't we dead yet?"

"He's curving around to set another shot at us, Billy. It
takes a while to turn one of those babies around. They're not
as agile as an F-16." Casey's chauvinism was showing; he was
a decided partisan of the little ultramaneuverable F-16 as op-
posed to the huge but fast F-15 Eagle.

"He's back at our eight o'clock, Lieutenant," Blum said.
"I think he's watching to see if we're going down."

"That's what we like to hear." Casey was skidding and slipping the airplane around, trying to make it look out of control. Gone was the laid-back California kid. In his place was a
curious clockwork creature, the Automated Pilot, hard and
precise: the consummate high-tech aerial killer.

"Casey, this is Jeff MacGregor," the speaker said in his
ear. "I know you're the best there is—but is there any chance
at all?"

"That's affirmative, Mr. President. She's unarmed and
she's slow and she's a big target. But she's maneuverable.
She's stressed like a fighter."

Blum looked up, pale. "No she isn't!"

Casey ignored him. "Hang on, sir," he rapped. He put the
nose down and dived through the cloud cover. Straight into
the middle of Baltimore.

"*Madre de dios!*" Olivarez yelped. A bronze building
loomed right in front of them, looking skeletal and strange
with all the window glass blown out by the blasts that had
racked the Washington area. Casey cranked her hard left
again, pulling six gees and making the graphite frame really
groan. The right wingtip sheered off against the metallic-
looking facade with a grinding screech.

Casey smiled.

"Missile launched!" Blum shouted. A moment later the

thunder of another explosion, near enough to rattle their teeth.

"What was that?" McKay demanded over the intercom.

"It hit the building, I think," Olivarez said.

Casey knew what had happened. The Eagle driver had gotten lazy, either thinking the Hercules was mortally wounded, or just plain figuring it had no chance to get away. When he'd realized what Casey had in mind, he'd punched off a second Sparrow radar-homing missile, hoping to nail the big bird before it lost itself in the steel and concrete canyons of the dead city, where his radar would never track it. Until the last millisecond it probably never occurred to him that the C-130's pilot would be insane enough to dive down through the cloud banks where only a personal act of God could ensure that they didn't smack a building right off.

But Casey Wilson wasn't insane. Nor was he just blowing in the breeze when he told the President they had a chance. It was a slim chance indeed, one that might have been shaved off with a surgeon's scalpel. But it was a chance.

Not crazy, Casey, but a man with literally nothing to lose by going for it. And he was the man who had almost flunked out of Air Combat Maneuvering school for being too aggressive and losing too many aircraft, until he found the energy-focusing disciplines of t'ai ch'i, and channeled his elemental drive for victory, controlled it. He was the perfect pilot, a natural-born stick-and-rudder man who had honed his raw abilities to the finest edge known to man, a genius of air combat. He knew this with the simple unconfounded newborn-baby arrogance of a true fighter pilot. Any combat jock had to think that way, if he wanted to make it.

In Casey's case it happened to be true.

And he did have some advantages. The Hercules' top speed was five hundred miles an hour—and they *parked* F-15s at that speed. On the other hand, even though the F-15 was astonishingly maneuverable for such a big fighter, the Super Hercules' winglets—those funny little fins on the wings McKay had found so humorous—enabled the big plane to amble along at scarcely any mph without stalling. And for all its amazingly ungainly appearance, the Hercules could turn as if one wingtip were nailed to the ground.

The Israelis had pegged it right, back when they dubbed the airplane the Hippo; it had the same stubby, almost comical appearance. But in its element, the water, a hippopotamus could move with panther speed and ballet dancer grace; and in the air the dumpy Herkie became similarly graceful.

The big bird wallowed like a boat in high seas. It was purely intentional; Casey actually had the plane down *among* the buildings, keeping toward the outskirts of the city center so that he could fly over the lower buildings and between the skyscrapers, constantly changing direction as much to avoid running smack into a building as to spoil the F-15 pilot's tracking solution.

In a moment he caught a glimpse of the Eagle through the portside windows. The big fighter was painted pale air-superiority gray, tough to spot against blue sky or cloud. It stood right out against the black building it had just come around, all its flaps extruded to dirty the airframe and kill speed. Even as he watched, white smoke billowed from under the Eagle's right wing.

Casey jerked the stick hard right, and howling with agony, the Hercules heeled over. He might as well have saved his effort.

Too close for the radar-seeking Sparrows to track—if he even had any left—the Eagle pilot had triggered a Sidewinder heatseeker instead. The problem with that little trick was that the engines of a propeller-driven aircraft don't give off much heat, and are hard to spot even for the keen infrared eye of the all-angle AIM-9 the F-15 fired. Also, the Super Herkie was blessed with an infrared-suppressive kit that cooled its exhaust and diffused it before letting it go—rendering it almost invisible to a heatseeker. The Sidewinder buzzed past on a miniature blue comet of flame, gone ballistic, to splash down somewhere in Chesapeake Bay. A moment later, wings level and throttle pushed forward to stave off an imminent stall, the F-15 howled across the Hercules' tail and vanished from view.

The cockpit crew breathed a collective sigh of relief. "That's three," Wu said sleepily. The right side of his flight suit was dyed crimson-purple with blood.

"They carry eight," Olivarez said grimly. His square, handsome face was dotted with little hemispheres of sweat.

"Maybe not," was all Casey said. Having been a wartime fighter jock, he knew munition resupply was a constant headache. The outbreak of war on the ground in Eastern Europe had almost certainly sucked North America dry of all but the barest few air-to-air missiles necessary to mount a skeletal air defense. Casey was willing to bet his life—and in effect was— that the Eagle was carrying at the max two Sidewinders and two of the larger radar-guided Sparrows. That would mean he was almost dry already. On the other hand, he still had the 20-millimeter cannon in the nose.

That worried Casey. He was a big fan of aerial gunfighting. Of his seven kills, three had been made with the 20-millimeter Gatling in the needle nose of his pet F-16, including two on his epic five-kill mission over Syria. He liked guns. They were simple, and you controlled them in person. They didn't respond to reflected radar pulses or their own heat vision, sensitive sensory and steering mechanisms whose complexity invited malfunction.

The sniper's rifle is an extension of his eyes, Jim Morrison had said, *he kills with injurious vision.* On the ground as in the air, that was how Casey fought.

And unfortunately no ground-clutter or ultracool-running engines would protect them from the evil eye of that Eagle driver.

Casey banked right, flew between a couple of hotels near the waterfront, over a white-tiered shopping structure that looked like someone's trashed wedding cake, and over the water, surging green-brown and sluggish under the clouds, then angled back in over the convention center, and finally took her back downtown.

No missiles had detonated due east of Baltimore, so most of the glass remained on the eastern faces of the buildings downtown—and this saved all their lives. Casey was looking at a weird reflection of the black Hercules hurtling on a collision course with itself in the glass of a skyscraper almost a kilometer ahead when he saw an angular flake of silver-gray ripple down behind it, and a sudden billow of white. The Eagle was back, and it had just fired another missile.

He "unloaded" the big airplane, pushing the nose down so it descended at the same rate a free object might fall. A few cars were rusting out on the roof of a five-story parking garage right in front of them, getting closer *fast*. Even as Olivarez turned the color of old parchment beside him, Casey pulled the stick to his belly.

The missile whistled overhead, straight down the Hercules' center line, and blew most of the glass off the skyscraper ahead. Car roofs crunched like eggshells beneath the Herkie's tires, and then the big blunt nose was up, the airplane clawing for altitude with its multibladed props.

—almost a fatal lapse of judgment on Casey's part. The Eagle jock was following his missile, straight and hot. The startled flight crew saw the fighter flash by in planform within fifteen meters of their nose, a sleek gray arrowhead of death. Jetwash slammed the Hercules' nose earthward toward buildings that reached for it like blunt concrete arms. Casey fought it up again, just clearing a Sheraton as the FSE pilot pitched up and grabbed sky in a patented F-15 seventy-degree climb. He was gone through the clouds almost instantly.

"That's four," Olivarez said. "Think he's going home?"

"No chance." Casey turned hard right to miss the building that had mirrored the F-15's pass. He'd hardly done so, it seemed, when the Eagle materialized through the clouds *dead ahead*, coming straight at them. It flashed by in an instant as the flight systems engineer cried out in alarm.

Casey chuckled. "Smart." The F-15 driver had pulled a 270-degree barrel roll. Had Casey broken left instead of right, the Eagle could have pulled a few gees and rolled out right on his tail, in perfect position for a gun-firing pass. But Casey's luck—or foresightedness—could only delay the inevitable. The Eagle was going to be back on his tail, sooner or later, raking him with his guns. Because of the F-15's stall speed, the fighter jock was never going to find himself in the enviable position of being trapped at his enemy's six o'clock position; he was going to have to overshoot sooner or later. But that wouldn't be as deadly as it usually was in air-to-air combat, since the Hercules had no forward-firing weapons to shoot him when he got out front—no weapons at all. But it was annoying. The Eagle was going to have to make pass after pass until his 20-millimeter shot the Hercules to pieces.

Casey knew all this. He just hoped the fighter jock got good and irritated—and that the Super Hercules held together until he got the chance to consummate the plan that had formed instantly in his mind when he realized they had been bounced by a fighter.

If only—

Weaving, Casey spotted the F-15, dropping through clouds and arrowing up on him from behind. He jinked, hauling the Hercules' big high tail from side to side as wildly as the airframe would allow, and then faster still. Came the rolling thunder of the Gatling in the F-15's nose. Tracers drifted past the windscreen, deceptively lazy and slow, looking as they always did like beg red flaming golfballs. Then the enemy pilot got his aim.

The Herkie jittered spastically as the enemy pumped slugs into the left wing. An instant of everything rattling, out of focus, and the quick fear, hot and quick as a flash fire, that the wing would go. And then the double orange glow of the Eagle's tailpipes out front, vanishing as the pilot cranked it around a building ahead of the Hercules.

Blum craned his neck. "Port inboard engine's smoking pretty badly, Lieutenant."

"Thank God she's a tough bird," Olivarez said.

Then the fighter was back, blitzing in on their eight o'clock, close in and blasting. The airplane shuddered violently as the 20-millimeter strikes walked up the Left wing, clawed through the fuselage. Mobile One rang with mind-busting noise as shells exploded against its hull. Sam Sloan's fingers tightened on the wheel until it seemed the white knuckles would pop out through the skin. At his side, an ashen-faced MacGregor winced at the hideous racket; Srinarampa, lashed into a folddown aft with his own belt, had his face buried in his hands. With no time to improvise straps of his own, McKay sat in another fold-down hanging onto brackets in the hull with all his strength, straining against the G-forces that pulled at him like monster hands.

The stream of metal found the cockpit. Casey's world filled up with flame and smoke and broken glass and deafening noise. After eternity, it passed.

There was fire in the cockpit. Olivarez called for the flight engineer to break out the extinguisher. No response. He twisted in his seat. Blum was clutching at the stump of his severed right arm with futile fingers and weeping. Wu slumped in his seat with his head lolled back and his eyes rolled into his head, stone dead. Olivarez unbuckled himself and hauled down the fire extinguisher himself, dousing the engineer's panel.

"Hold together, baby," Casey murmured. "Just a few more seconds."

As he fought the flames down, the copilot noticed that the plane was climbing. Dropping the extinguisher, he hurled himself forward to stare out the windscreen as Casey broke through the cloud cover like a sounding whale. Wildly he looked at the pilot. Casey was looking straight ahead, his face fixed in a strange heat-shrunk grin.

"Are you insane?" Olivarez shrieked.

Impossibly, the grin tightened a notch. "Third time's the charm," Casey said, as if to himself. "He's getting pissed."

Like a leaping shark the F-15 broke the cloud cover in a forty-five-degree climb two klicks to their left. Casey banked slowly right, and Olivarez groaned—they were going *away* from the sleek killer, a maneuver practically guaranteed to pull him in on their tail.

Black smoke billowing from the inboard left engine eclipsed the fighter. A quick glance at the panel up front showed a solid blaze of red. Almost all of the primary systems that could malfunction were malfunctioning, and a lot of the secondaries were none too healthy. The starboard outside engine was just plain gone. Hydraulics were feeble, electrics complaining and there were fires in the cargo compartment. If they weren't brought under control quickly, the airplane would burn up. But that was academic, since Casey had pulled the Hercules around in a wide looping *slooow* turn. Olivarez caught a glimpse of an intact radar screen that showed the unmistakable blip of the F-15 in their six o'clock position, seven klicks out and closing fast.

And Casey—suicidally, America's premier fighter pilot was in a slow, shallow, straight dive. "Are you crazy?" Olivarez shouted again. He wanted to clutch Casey's arm, but something held him back. He felt this sudden strange sensation of *déjà vu,* as if he'd been here before . . . something about the lay of the land, the sparkle of sun on sea far away off to their right.

The clouds swallowed them. And suddenly the airplane was on its right side, and Olivarez could *feel* the wings starting to tear away at the roots, and the blood draining from behind his eyes, and that huge bronze building was gleaming *right in front of them.* There was a thumping crash as the Hercules' landing gear kissed the side of the building, and then they were away, leveling out.

The F-15 driver had had them dead to rights. He had seen the enemy pilot obviously losing control of his waddling four-engined beast, obviously befuddled by the lightning ferocity of the Eagle's attack. Now the Herkie was giving him a perfect shot at its tail, not even bothering to dodge. A good thing, too; the Eagle driver was sick of fucking with the sons of bitches. That bastard flying the Herkie had already kept him too long from a cool drink at the officers' club—and the thousand ounces of gold Chairman Maximov was offering for Vice President MacGregor and each of the Guardians.

The FSE pilot pulled up several hundred meters, then dropped the nose, unloaded into a gentle dive, pushed the throttle to full military. He opened fire from extreme range even as the Hercules disappeared back into the cloudbank like a frightened dog scooting under a hedge.

It was time to end this.

It was. The Eagle's airspeed indicator was quivering at .8 mach when the plane broke through the bottom. A skyscraper stretched before him like a great golden cliff. He just had time to throw up his hands and scream when he struck. Blazing like a meteor, the fighter plunged at a slant through three floors before disintegrating into pieces too small to break through walls.

Battered, limping, burning—dying by centimeters—the Hercules continued its turn on into the south, toward Washington, D.C.

CHAPTER
TWENTY

Somehow Casey landed the shattered Hercules in the parking lot of a derelict cement plant twenty klicks northwest of the capital. The tires hadn't been helped by bouncing them off car tops and buildings, and about half of them blew on landing; the big plane completed the last half of its taxi to rest skidding broadside in huge clouds of blue rubber smoke.

After the battering they had taken, Sam and Casey and McKay and Tom were barely able to get down the rear hatch and unfasten Mobile One. The chains which held it had snapped; only the taffy-like windings of elastic had kept it in place during the landing.

The men all looked like hell. MacGregor's sprained arm was already bound across his chest by the ever-solicitous Tom Rogers. Rogers himself sported a swollen mouth and cracked teeth from having bounced his face off the receivers of his turret guns. Dr. Srinarampa was still dazed and logy from the blow that had left half his face a purple-black bruise. Every one of them was so thoroughly battered he could barely move. But they did it. They undogged the car and drove it out onto the cracked, weed-grown cement.

Immediately they opened every hatch. "Sloan," McKay

said, "I'm going to give you shit about this till the end of your days. You, of all the goddamned people in the world, getting seasick and spitting up all over the place."

Sloan's face was still greenish gray. "It's airsick, not seasick. I've never been in a ship that pitched like that, not even a destroyer in a North Atlantic storm!"

"If you gentlemen don't mind," Jeff MacGregor said, gagging slightly, "could we talk about something else?"

Olivarez refused to leave the airplane or his dead comrades. They were all dead, Flight Engineer Blum having bled to death before he could be helped. What the copilot was going to do next—shift for himself, surrender to an expeditionary force patrol, try against reason to get the smoking, sagging wreck skyborne again, or just waste away and die—they didn't know. They just left him in the gathering twilight. There was nothing they could do, and the mission was breathing down their necks.

They used what water they could spare to sluice out the vehicle's interior on the roll. It still stank, but there was nothing they could do for that. Under the cloud cover the day was hot and close as a wet suit. "Where now?" Casey Wilson asked from the driver's seat. He was still displaying an incipient shit-eating grin. It wasn't everyday somebody killed one of the world's finest fighter aircraft with an unarmed cargo plane.

"Washington," McKay said. "Where else?"

All roads led to D.C. and all roads were hell. It took them until full dark to get to the outskirts of D.C. And if the roads were hell, what they met when they crossed the Beltway—

Stalled cars in profusion; go around or bulldoze through. Streets choked with rubble so deep the straining car could barely scale the mounds, treacherous ground that threatened to swallow them with every meter. Blocks of burned-out buildings. As lush in wreckage as the Amazon Basin was in greenery.

And the people, denizens of the blackest pit of hell. Glimpses now and again of forms flitting through ruins, staring from cavern storefronts, gazing down from rooftops. Many shouted obscenities or hurled rocks and bottles impotently against the steel and titanium hide of Mobile One. Occasional shots flashed from the dark, ricocheted harmlessly off the hull; once a rocket fired from a third story etched a line of sparks right in front of the car's nose. Tom Rogers hosed the front of the building it had come from with lead and white phosphorous death. A shrieking, blazing figure staggered out of the tentacles of white smoke, pitched into a pile of rubble, lay thrashing. They drove on.

Once a mob confronted them, shouting angry faces, hands and boards and bits of rubble pounding on the hull. Torches waved like banners of flame; the occupants of the car looked in all directions for the orange meteor of a Molotov coming their way.

They weren't disappointed. McKay was looking out the portside viewslit above the firing port, when a gasoline bomb arced in from the left and behind and splashed right below the firing port. McKay jerked back reflexively with a curse. "Goose her, Case, get us out of here!"

Casey cast one bleak look back at McKay. There were dozens of people crowded in front of them, pressed together solidly against the car.

McKay chanced another glance outside the port. A filter of fire danced before his eyes. There didn't seem any way it was going to get inside, though he sure as hell wasn't going to stick his head out to check unless it became absolutely necessary. But he would take no chances with the President's life—not with their goal practically in sight.

"Casey—go for it!" Casey gulped and hit the accelerator.

People screamed as their bodies squashed beneath the tires of the mammoth car. McKay heard a thump, a bang, a hissing explosion as Tom Rogers unloaded a CS hand grenade out the top hatch of the turret. That thinned the crowd away some. Then Rogers let loose a long ripping burst over their heads from the turret guns and they fled in all directions. Casey sped ahead. His cocky air of triumph had vanished.

Through the long, hot, deadly night they drove. And then they were slanting down New York Avenue, miraculously clear of cars and rubble, between the Treasury and the Treasury Annex, and there were figures stirring sleepily around guttering campfires among bare trees in Lafayette Park, and on the left—

Battered and blackened, caved in in places, but still, miraculously intact: the White House. McKay gripped Casey's shoulder. "Go for it! Hit it hard!"

A muzzle flash blossomed from the darkness of the park, another, then a ragged volley, full-auto fire rippling across a handful of single shots. Rogers's M-19 boomed response. Grenades made fire-fountains of the trampled mud that had once been pampered turf.

Brakes locked, the car skidded to a halt before the main entrance. Even McKay appreciated the irony; the last time they had seen this battered portico had been under similar circumstances—hunkered down and taking fire as the mobs attacked after the all-clear sounded.

Tom Rogers returned fire among the trees of the North Lawn while Casey turned the car around in its tracks so McKay and Sloan, supporting the President between them, could bail out the side. They ran up the steps of the White House, a bewildered Dr. Srinarampa trotting at their heels, McKay blazing into the night one-handed with his M-60 machine gun, Sloan humping his Galil-203 combo.

Bullets cracked about them, throwing stinging sprays of marble chips into their hands and faces, and then they were in the entranceway, where year-old skeletons still sprawled on the faded, water-stained carpet. Casey goosed the vehicle through another one-eighty and dived for the new subterranean-garage exit that led in under the West Wing, so that Tom Rogers could fire up the snipers from a hull-down position.

Inside the building was deserted, empty, dead. There was no sign of life anywhere, inside or on the North or South Lawns. It was as if the gangs that warred for control of the wreckage of Washington had by mutual unspoken agreement decided to leave the grounds sacrosanct. As Sam Sloan hustled the President to relative safety downstairs, McKay tore through closet storage on the ground floor in a frantic search. In a matter of moments he found what he was looking for, dashed for the stairs.

A hailstorm of gunfire greeted McKay's solitary figure as it emerged on the third-floor promenade. Ignoring the shots ricocheting all around, he moved to the center of the facade, hurriedly but purposefully. The shooters out in the park redoubled their efforts.

Then as dawn cracked the eastern horizon, the first sunlight of the Fourth of July fell across the flag of the United States as it unfurled from the White House flagpole. The snipers ceased their barrage, momentarily awestruck as they saw the flag of their country flying from that spot for the first time in a year.

McKay stood beside it, proud in his brief moment of emotional defiance. For him, America . . . had come home.